Managing Health and Safety

Learning Made Simple

Managing
Health and Safety

Learning Made Simple

Jacqueline Jeynes

Routledge
Taylor & Francis Group

LONDON AND NEW YORK

First Published 2007 by Butterworth-Heinemann

Published 2015 by Routledge
2 Park Square, Milton Park, Abingdon, Oxon, OX14 4RN
711 Third Avenue, New York, NY 10017

Routledge is an imprint of the Taylor & Francis Group, an informa business

Notice
No responsibility is assumed by the publisher for any injury and/or damage to
persons or property as a matter of products liability, negligence or otherwise, or from
any use or operation of any methods, products, instructions or ideas contained in the
material herein.

British Library Cataloguing in Publication Data
A catalogue record for this book is available from the British Library.

Library of Congress Cataloguing in Publication Data
A catalogue record for this book is available
from the Library of Congress.

ISBN: 978-0-7506-8441-5

Edited and typeset by P.K. McBride

Cartoons by John Leech

Icons designed by Sarah Ward © 1994

Contents

Preface

Managing health and safety effectively in the workplace is often seen as the responsibility of a designated 'expert'. However, everyone in the organisation has responsibility for making sure their actions do not cause harm or injury to others. It is vital, therefore, that everyone understands their role in managing health and safety risks

This Learning Made Simple guide outlines the basic principles that underpin effective health and safety management, identifying hazards, assessing risks and making sure adequate controls are in place to safeguard people from harm. It assumes the reader has experience in a workplace, perhaps with some basic health and safety risk awareness.

It is intended to help the reader identify hazards and risks associated with their own workplace, making sure that they (and other workers) take appropriate actions to eliminate or reduce these risks. While it covers the main elements associated with *managing* H&S in certificate or diploma courses such as those offered by NEBOSH and CIEH for instance, it does not cover specific regulations in detail.

It is primarily a practical tool to help team leaders, supervisors and managers ensure their own health and safety as well as that of others in their team. I hope that you find it useful in your workplace.

Dr Jacqueline Jeynes

2007

1 Start here

Introduction

Many people refer to Health & Safety as commonsense and say there is too much regulation. To some extent, this is a reasonable statement, but it is also true that one person's commonsense is not the same as another's – it develops over time as you experience life at home and at work.

Everyone perceives risk in a different way, depending on age, life experiences, health and safety expertise, skills and, in some cases, gender.

Case study

In January 2007 several companies were found guilty of failing to ensure the safety of a worker who fell to his death through a roof light when working on a fragile asbestos cement roof.

The HSE (Health and Safety Executive) brought the prosecution, stating: "It was only Mr Moran's second day and he had not worked on a site before. He had been given no training or protection and was paid cash in hand. It was a shambles of a job."

If you run a business, or work for a company where you have some responsibility for health and safety, you cannot rely on the presumed commonsense of others to keep everyone safe from harm or injury.

Health and Safety Management covers the main principles of good occupational health and safety (OH&S) management including risk assessment, responsibilities and typical ways to record your findings.

There may be particular hazards in your workplace that need more formal assessment by a specialist – for example, air monitoring or fibre sampling and testing – but the basic principles should allow you to establish a sound system for managing OH&S risks in your workplace.

Managing health and safety

When we talk about managing health and safety effectively, we are really talking about making sure people are protected from harm or injury when they are at work, whether they are workers or visitors to the workplace. Because it relates to work activities, it is often referred to as occupational health and safety (OH&S).

H&S regulations do not apply to domestic premises unless you are:

◆ A professional carer or peripatetic worker (someone who travels to see clients in their own premises).

◆ A homeworker for a company that requires you to work away from your normal workplace at times, e.g. performing administrative tasks via a networked computer system.

◆ A homeworker (sometimes called an outworker) paid solely on the basis of carrying out tasks from your own home premises, e.g. making clothing or packing individual greetings cards.

◆ A self-employed individual who is working in someone else's domestic premises, or works from home.

Some domestic staff may be covered by the regulations, although members of the family working in a business may not be. The law is a bit confusing in these circumstances, so you should check the legal position on an individual basis.

 OH&S legislation is there to protect the health and safety of people. Although this includes a wide range of risks, other legislation exists to cover similar or additional risks, such as food safety, environmental protection or product safety.

To manage OH&S effectively, you need to:

◆ Take a structured, logical approach to identify risks.

◆ Decide the best way to control these risks.

◆ Establish systems and procedures to record and monitor how you are managing risks so that you can demonstrate this to others.

People covered by OH&S law

The law is there to protect people from injury or harm when at work, and anyone who may be affected by work activities. This includes:

- Employees of the firm, including full-time or part-time, temporary or permanent staff and casual workers.

- Volunteers who work alongside paid staff, e.g. in a charity shop.

- Students or young people on work experience.

- Contractors and sub-contractors.

- Self-employed individuals including those working on their own behalf as sole traders (who may employ other people).

- Peripatetic workers not based in one location.

- Drivers and transport staff.

- Clients or customers in your premises.

- People in the surrounding area who may be affected by the work activities – e.g., noisy processes, toxic emissions, or transporting potentially harmful materials.

- Other visitors to your premises, whether they are legally entitled to be there or not, such as intruders on an old, unsafe roof.

Insurance

Your insurance provider may want to see records of accidents, injuries, previous claims, staff training, fire drills and other documents related to how you control risks before they decide the premium to charge. If you supply goods or services to other businesses, they may want to see evidence of your OH&S management system before they will enter into a contract with you.

The stakeholders

All the different groups of people listed represent the stakeholders in your business, the people who have a stake in (might be affected by) the way you choose to deal with OH&S risks. Other stakeholders who want to know that you are managing the risks effectively include:

◆ the regulators, inspectors from the Health & Safety Executive (HSE) or Environmental Health Officers (EHO);

◆ your insurance provider, particularly if you work in an industry with a high risk of accidents, such as agriculture or construction;

◆ Trades Union representatives and other worker representatives who need to ensure their members are adequately protected.

Basically, you need to show them that you:

1 have identified the current situation;

2 have identified problem areas that need to be addressed;

3 have dealt with them appropriately;

4 can demonstrate what actions have been taken;

5 are in control of the situation.

Activity: The benefits of managing OH&S effectively

Think about the following questions for a moment.

Q1: Why is it important to be seen to manage health and safety effectively?

Q2: What are the consequences likely to be if you get it wrong?

If you have little or no experience of dealing with OH&S, it can seem a daunting task to establish a system for managing risks on a day-to-day basis. However, there are likely to be some elements of a system in place already, so it is more a case of drawing these together in a coherent way rather than starting from scratch. However small your organisation, the EHO or HSE inspector will expect to see evidence of an OH&S system.

I don't know why we have to do risk assessments...

Case study

A substantial fine was imposed on a theme park owner after an all-terrain vehicle rolled over and passengers were thrown into a river. Health and safety management was poor. The driver had only been shown how to drive the vehicle the day before, the route had not been checked for dangerous conditions following bad weather, the vehicle was not sufficiently padded to cushion the impact, seatbelts were found to be ineffective, and height restrictions for children were not adhered to. Such bad publicity will hit sales, as customers will not feel safe. Future insurance premiums will also be affected.

Answers to questions (page 5)

Q1. The benefits for the organisation from getting the OH&S system right:

- It will help to protect people from personal injury or harm, reduce sickness absences and contribute to a healthier workforce.

- Reducing accidents will be reflected in lower insurance premiums.

- More efficient use of resources, using safer alternatives to substances, better maintenance of machinery reduces noise impact and can reduce costs associated with scrap and waste disposal.

- Good public relations with customers and the local community, help staff recruitment and retention, or increase sales.

- And, of course, you must comply with legislation.

Q2. The consequences of getting it wrong:

- Possible death and injury for workers, customers or others, e.g. a passer-by hit by falling debris while you are repairing a roof.

- Long-term harm to workers, such as hearing loss, or damage to shoulder due to awkward repetitive movements when loading.

- Prosecution resulting in fines or imprisonment and bad publicity.

- Costs of hold-up in trading activities following an incident are unlikely to be fully covered by insurance.

- Higher insurance premiums, or refusal to provide cover.

- Loss of trade if you cannot meet contract requirements as a supplier.

- Problems with recruiting and retaining skilled staff, with potential for additional costs if you have to use agency or temporary staff.

The impact

The impact of an accident in the workplace is far-reaching, affecting:

* The individual injured or killed, and their family.

* Colleagues who witness an incident may need time off to recover.

* A stop on the machine or process while investigations take place.

* Time and costs associated with the investigation itself.

* Cost of fines, compensation, increased insurance premiums, sick pay and extra salaries.

* Fines and/or imprisonment, and subsequent criminal record for individuals in the firm who may be held responsible.

2 The initial review

Assess the current situation

Every organisation is different, with different types of hazards and range of measures in place to control risks. There may be a formal system in place (see page 89) with named individuals responsible for different elements of managing OH&S. Alternatively, there may be a much more flexible and informal approach, with few written records of risk assessments in place.

It is important to carry out an initial review, or audit if a formal OH&S management system is in place, to assess the current situation before taking further action. If there are other people in the organisation who have some responsibility for health and safety, they will obviously be a good starting point. Where possible, it is better to involve others in this review, and certainly let everyone know what you are doing and why so that they don't start getting jumpy!

Well, Mr. Giles, your risk assessments all seem to be up-to-date –
now if you'll just escort me to my car...

1 Start by identifying records, systems and procedures related to health and safety that are already in place. These might include:

- A copy of company Health & Safety Policy and any other statements, such as the Annual Report.

- The Employee Handbook and information provided during Induction Training.

- Other records of training, especially in H&S or specialist skills for working with certain processes or materials.

- Accident Book and First Aid records.

- Sickness absence records.

- Insurance documents and claim history.

- Names of people responsible for a specified element of health and safety, at any level in the organisation.

- Hazard Data Sheets (supplied by the manufacturer of substances) for products that may cause harm if not handled correctly.

- Risk Assessments already carried out and results recorded.

- Written Safe Systems of Work or details of specific skills required for certain tasks.

- Action plans to deal with any emergency situation.

2 Where is the information located and is it easily accessible? It can be in hard copy or electronic format and should be available for an inspector to see if they visit your premises.

Show you are managing risk

You must be able to demonstrate to stakeholders that you are managing risks effectively, so you need to keep records that show you have assessed risks, put controls in place, taken action to remedy situations where necessary, and that you monitor systems regularly to ensure they are working adequately.

Oh, Mr. Sykes is on the phone at the moment. If you would like to wait in reception he'll bring the records along in a minute.

Record keeping

You are required by law to record significant findings of risk assessments. If you employ five or more people, you must have a written health and safety policy plus records of the way you control risks and safeguard people from harm. Even if you only employ one person, you must record the findings of fire risk assessments.

Using a flow chart

There are two main areas to focus on when carrying out an initial review and subsequent risk assessments:

◆ The flow of products or people through the business.

◆ Physical elements of the location itself.

A simple flow chart can show where materials come in → the processes they go through to the final product → storage and distribution.

Flow chart 1: Manufacturing

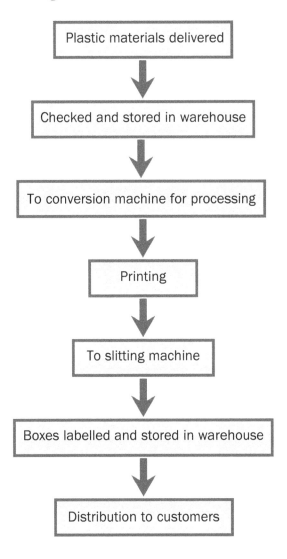

Flowchart 2: Service industry (hotel)

If it is a service industry, the flowchart can show all the points where contact is made with the customer and the type of activities that take place at these points.

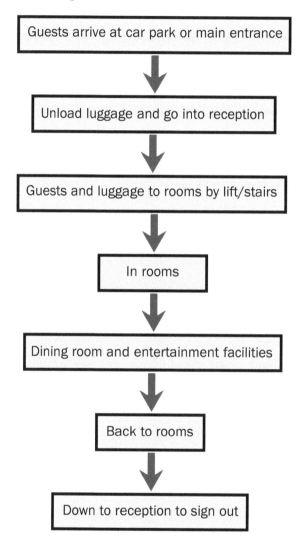

Even if the business is primarily IT/Internet based, or you work from home, and contact with clients is extremely limited, it is still important to consider the activities in your work space, where your materials are delivered and stored, and any rest facilities available.

If the work activities are carried out in someone else's premises, the contact points can still be identified in the flowchart even if they cannot easily be linked to a specific location.

Using a site plan

The physical layout of the business premises will have a potential impact on the range and type of hazards that are likely to be present.

It is much easier to identify risks systematically throughout the business by using a site plan. It can be an existing one provided by the landlord, for instance, or a hand-drawn sketch. It does *not* have to be to scale or produced by a qualified draughtsperson, but it does need to be big enough to record all the places where hazards may be present – A4 or A3 size is ideal.

Check your boundaries

If you own or lease the premises, you should have a copy of the boundary lines for land and buildings, including shared or communal areas. You should be able to get a copy from your landlord, solicitor, or try the local authority planning office website for your area.

Once you have the basic outline plan of the site, use 2 or 3 photocopies of it to record details, or try acetate sheets/tracing paper over the top of the outline plan.

Recording details of the site

Show the main features of the site as a whole – you might want to use the checklist to make notes or comments, such as communal or shared areas.

- External boundary of land.
- Roads and footpaths.
- Access routes for vehicles and pedestrians.
- External walls of all buildings, including sheds or outbuildings.
- Car park areas.
- Delivery areas.

Keep a copy of this basic outline for future use in sections on health and fire hazards.

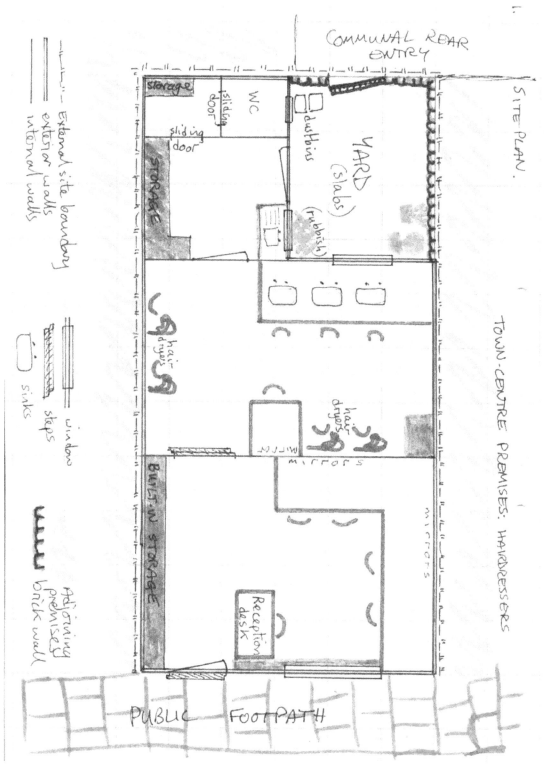

Sample site plan 1: Town centre premises.

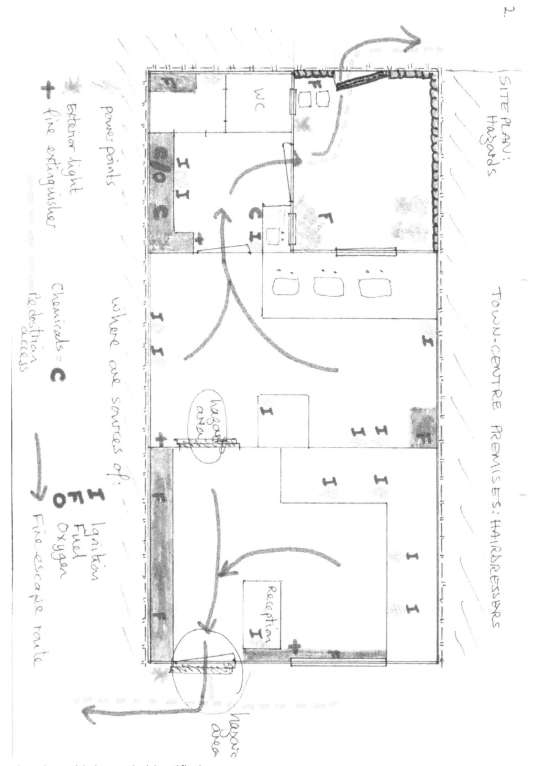

The site plan with hazards identified

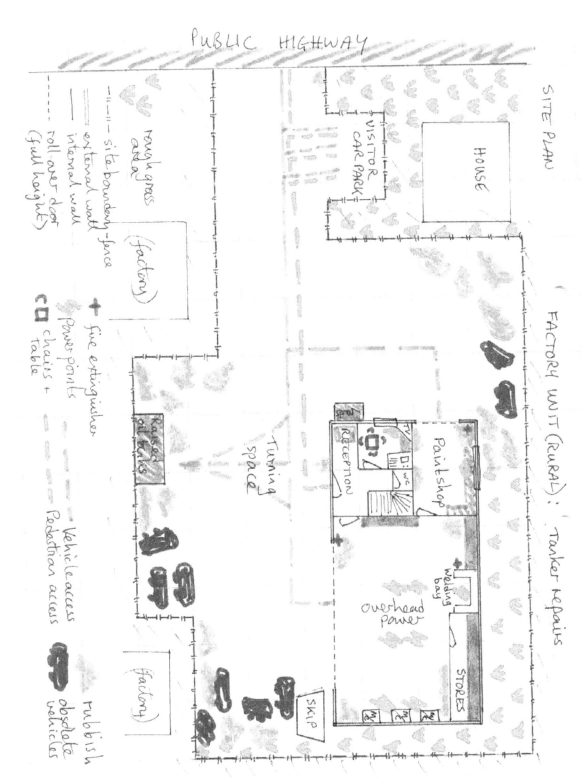

Sample site plan 2: Factory unit

18

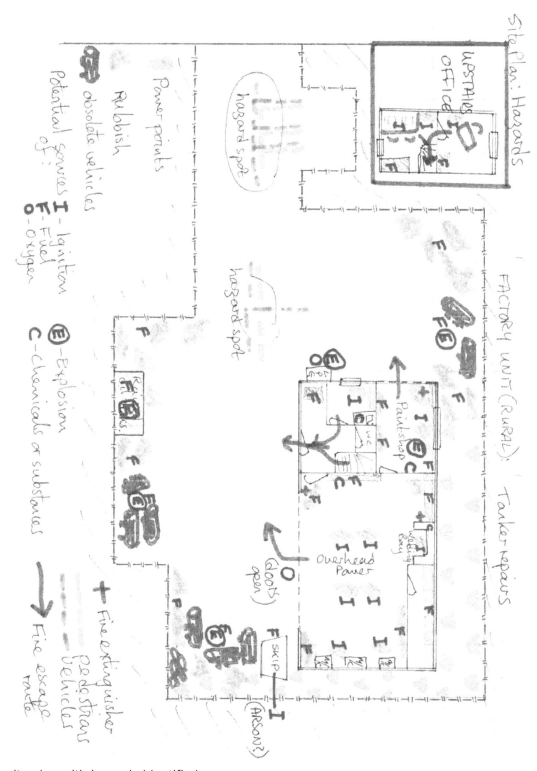

The site plan with hazards identified

Checklist 1: Site plan – summary list of features

Noted	Query?	Action needed
External boundary		
Access for vehicles (roads, tracks, etc.)		
Access for pedestrians (footpaths, etc.)		
Position of external walls of main building		
Position of sheds, outbuildings, etc.		
Exterior doors, windows identified		
Car park areas		
Delivery areas		

External features of the site

Add more details of external features, either directly to your plan or on tracing paper/acetate overlay. Are there any areas where you already know action is needed to make it safer? Consider these points – use the checklist to ensure you cover everything:

For visitors to the site

Is entry to the site clearly marked for both vehicles and pedestrians?

Is the reception area or main entrance to the building clearly identified, so that people are not wandering around looking for the way in?

Is it clear which entrances are NOT for visitors?

Where are lights positioned? Are they adequate? Working? Sufficient for the area being lit? Any very dark spots or areas in deep shadow? Note where lights are positioned on buildings and in other areas.

Vehicles

Are parking and turning areas clearly marked and kept free of obstacles?

Is it clear where short-term stops can be made, e.g. for deliveries?

Identify routes usually taken by fork-lift trucks, tractors or similar vehicles on site during normal working.

Surface of routes – make a note of any areas that are very poor and thus present a significant hazard to vehicles or pedestrians, such as vehicles overturning or people tripping.

Pedestrians

Are pedestrians separate from vehicle routes? Draw access routes on the plan, and crossing points where there should be painted lines or barriers.

Are there kerb edges or steps that people need to negotiate, and if so are they well maintained and secure? Identify any badly broken sections of paving, or step edges.

Where are lights positioned in relation to these steps – any changes or additions needed?

If you were a visitor to the site, maybe a sales representative or customer, and unfamiliar with it, what would be your first impressions as you walk around?

Excellent, I particularly like the way you have marked out this DANGER area...

Other external features:

Waste skips and dustbins – where are they in relation to the building, are they easily accessible by workers even when weather is poor? Is access restricted to unauthorised people, such as vandals or people dumping rubbish? Crucially, is the skip the right type for the waste being disposed of – you should be separating out different types of waste for collection.

LPG and other flammable substance storage, e.g. ink stores – are products stored appropriately according to suppliers' instructions/in safe, secure purpose-built cages or buildings? Add them to your Plan, and if you are not sure about any of these points then mark them for ation, and check with suppliers.

Storage tanks for water, oil, etc. - again, include them on the plan, noting whether they are appropriate, adequate, secure and well maintained. Identify whether you have sole responsibility for such storage, or it is joint responsibility with others.

Add features that may now be considered permanent but which are removable such as waste bits and pieces collected over time; obsolete vehicles, equipment, or machinery that may have been kept 'for spares' (but will never be used!); damaged pallets or shelving/racking that should either be sent back to the suppliers or disposed of.

Apart from the fire hazards these features represent, which we will look at more closely later, there are always the safety hazards of people tripping and being injured, rubbish piling up haphazardly with the possibility of falling, and of course poor visibility or obstructions for people driving on site.

Is your documentation accessible?

It is important to make sure relevant documentation related to managing OH&S risks is collated and easily accessible. If documents are in electronic format, make sure password-controlled access is not exclusive to just one person.

Checklist 2: External features summary list

Noted	Query?	Action needed
Signs for visitors		
Lights around site, on buildings		
Vehicle turning areas		
Parking including short-term areas		
Regular routes for fork-lift trucks and other vehicles		
Poor surfaces; kerbs and steps for pedestrians		
Waste skips; dustbins; areas where rubbish or waste materials deposited		
LPG, chemicals, flammable substances stores		
Storage tanks, for water, oil, or other liquids		
Obsolete machinery, equipment, vehicles, pallets, etc.		
Security: perimeter gates and fences		
Security: lights and CCTV		
Power lines and fuse boxes outside		
Roof details		

Security

Although not specifically an element of health and safety protection, security can play a major part in managing risks. There might be very little in the way of security, with no restriction to access or control of movement through the site. Security lights, and window or gate locks may also be absent. You can get specific guidance on security measures you need, but you do need to be clear what you want to secure the premises against, for example trespass, burglary, theft, vandalism, arson or access to sensitive material.

Whatever the purpose of your security measures, some of the points you might consider include:

- Perimeter access - walls, fences, gates.
- Control of vehicles and people on site.
- Security lights, CCTV.
- Locking devices on doors, windows, storage areas.

The building structures

Aspects of the building structure itself may present potential hazards, such as external power lines or fuse boxes, either as a source of danger when accessed illegally, or as overhanging cables across routes used by large vehicles.

Roofs are critical, whether you are in single or two or three storey buildings. The main problems are ease of access to burglars; adequate access to and maintenance of damaged areas; and how fragile the roof surface itself is (for example, old corrugated asbestos sheets).

Internal features of buildings and work areas

If people work on more than one floor, you need an outline for each unless the layout and activities are virtually identical. For fire risk assessments, there should be a separate floor plan for each.

Include all internal walls, passageways, doors and stairs. Also include fixed storage racking/shelving and workbenches, but use a different symbol for each. If portable shelving is used to divide working areas, then include that too.

In a manufacturing firm, overhead power supplies and large pieces of machinery should be identified, as should computer terminals in an office environment. Identify toilet, washing and eating areas, as well as the main large pieces of furniture, equipment or machinery.

Also note where fire extinguishers, smoke alarms, fire exits are located add a red '?' if they are missing or not working. A photograph of each work area or section would be invaluable here, with details of:

♦ Main activities carried out.

♦ Where machinery and equipment is used and stored.

♦ The usual position of desks, tables, chairs, computers, shelving, tills and so on.

Checklist 3: Internal features – Summary list

Noted	Query?	Action needed
Plan for each floor of premises		
Internal walls		
Stairs		
Doors, including sliding or folding doors		
Fixed storage shelves or racks		
Portable storage		
Fixed workbenches or surfaces		
Overhead power supplies		
Large pieces of equipment or machinery		
Large pieces of furniture		
Computers or IT equipment		
Toilet and washing facilities		
Eating areas, kitchens, vending machines		
Fire extinguishers and smoke alarms		

Consult the employees

Whatever size the organisation, you must have procedures for consulting with employees on health and safety issues. In a small firm, this may just mean talking to all workers together. In a larger one, you might need to consult through a smaller group, including elected representatives of the workforce. If there is a trade union, there will probably already be a system in place. Consulting means discussing health and safety issues directly with the people who are affected by them – not just passing on details of decisions already made without their input.

Identify activities that take place on site

Use the flow chart and site plans to identify what activities take place in each area of the site. If you can, walk around the site, talk to people who work there, and make a note of any concerns you or they have.

How many people regularly work in each area?

Are there contractors on site sometimes, and if so which areas do they have access to?

Do you use temporary staff occasionally, and if so what do they do and where do they work?

Do people sleep on site?

Identify any staff that work alone in an area (especially if there are fewer people working on some late shifts), young workers or any staff with physical impairment such as hearing/sight loss or restricted mobility.

Make notes about the type of activity taking place in each area, including regular tasks and those that only occur occasionally – especially maintenance or large-scale cleaning jobs. Include workers who drive or travel for business purposes and only visit the site occasionally, plus those that work mainly from home.

A checklist that identifies the following elements is useful:

Area	Activities taking place	Equipment used	No of people involved

Things to look for

Arrival on site

Do visitors have to sign in when they arrive? How do you monitor movement of visitors on site, especially if there are restricted areas that are particularly dangerous or sensitive?

If you are a service provider, where do clients enter and wait to see you? Is there a procedure for signing in and out? How do you know that people have arrived, where they are waiting, the route by which they will leave after their appointments?

Virtually all businesses receive deliveries of goods or materials, if only the mail. It may be an extremely minor element of your particular business, just requiring a couple of sentences to acknowledge that you have thought about it. On the other hand, there may be quite a wide range of people coming to your premises to collect or deliver items, so they may represent additional hazards such as:

◆ Vehicles unattended, sometimes with doors open.

◆ Loading/unloading goods – do staff help sometimes?

◆ What the driver of the vehicle is responsible for, especially if they are employed by another firm – what they can or cannot do.

◆ Special equipment available to transport items from the point of delivery, either by hand or with a trolley/truck.

Goods are often delivered on standard-sized pallets, but smaller quantities may be delivered in containers of all shapes and sizes. How are contents checked, where and how are deliveries stacked on site at the time of delivery?

Storage of goods

Supplies: identify where goods arrive, where they are stored, and how they get to where they have to be used. Adequate storage space and facilities may be an issue, such as boxes of stationery stored on the ground floor when delivered, but actually used upstairs. This will generate more journeys up and down stairs, which means greater likelihood of tripping or falling.

Having identified storage areas on the site plans, identify what sort of stacking systems are in place, how storage areas are secured, and what control there is over access to them.

Hazardous substances include solvents, inks, bleach-based products, poisons and some cleaning agents. Even if you only use small amounts, there may be special requirements for how and where they are stored, whether they should be kept in special containers, what they are stored next to, and whether they should be kept at certain temperatures.

This does not include food or perishable items, although these may be an issue for some firms – whether it is to feed staff, a saleable commodity, or will be processed in some way. Some products, such as flour, can represent a significant risk to health (affecting the lungs and chest when particles are breathed in) and safety (as particles in the atmosphere burn easily and spread flames rapidly over a large area). At this stage though, we are focusing on potential hazards associated with storing goods.

Reception area

Often overlooked, the reception area can also be an area for concern. There may not be a receptionist in attendance all of the time, so you need to consider whether there is a procedure for signing in and out of the premises, and to provide health, safety and fire risk information to visitors.

Once people are on site, where do they sit and wait, are refreshments available, and is access to some parts of the site restricted to them?

Example: Waiting for repairs

Drivers who deliver vehicles for repair may have to wait for some time. They can sit in a designated area, but it is very dirty and scruffy, chairs have unsuitable stuffing (fire hazard) – in fact, very depressing! So they become bored and wander into the workshop to see what is happening, and talk to people carrying out repairs. Clearly this is unsatisfactory, and despite notices being displayed around the area telling them it is not acceptable, no-one actually enforces it.

Work progress through firm

Using the flow chart and site plans, note work areas or sections for goods or services as they move through the business. Don't forget to include activities that take place outside the building. It is easier to use another copy of the plan or additional tracing paper/acetate overlay to show the following:

Materials coming out of stores and going on to the first process stage – what do people do with them, how are they transferred to next stage? Are they easily moved as on a conveyor belt; does someone turn around and pass it on to the next person; does someone have to carry it?

When it has completed all the stages, how does it get to the customer – is it stored while waiting for collection? Packaging processes can use complex or hazardous equipment, including staple guns and cling-wrap machines.

In a service industry, the customer may be the 'Work in progress' in that they move from one work area to another, so using the same principles, where do they go at each stage? In the same way, when you go to another businesses' site or the customer's home, you must be alert to the same sort of questions.

If there are procedures already in place for any of these stages, check:

◆ Whether they are written down.

◆ When they were put together.

◆ Whether they are still workable, relevant, and safe.

◆ Whether they need to be amended (which means you will have to look at them to check!).

 Check existing procedures for arrival and departure of visitors; movement of vehicles on site; how goods in and goods out are monitored; how people pass on goods to next stage in the process. If you have a formal quality system in place, it should reflect these procedures.

If there are large or complex pieces of machinery in use, there may be formal 'safe system of work', or specified 'permit to work' procedures in place. Collect all the documents together so that you can access them readily when needed.

EXAMPLE completed Checklist 4: Activities the take place

Area	Activities	Equipment used	No of people
Reception	Take deliveries Meet visitors & sign them in Make tea & coffee Use phone/VDU	VDU Telephone & switchboard Kettle & coffee machine	1
Waiting and rest area	Tea, coffee, lunches Customers can watch TV	Kettle and microwave TV	4 max
Main shopfloor	Remove engine covers Check vehicle components & structure Fit replacement parts	Hoist; compressed air; overhead drilling & riveting tools; portable electrical equipment; LPG; trolleys and trucks	3
Welding bay and paint shop	MIG/gas welding Spray paint bodywork Spot repairs by hand Spray clean vehicles when necessary	Welding equipment Compressed air lines Hand-held tools	2
Office	Admin and secretarial Filing Talking to customers by phone	Computers/ VDU Printer, photocopier Telephone	1
Stores	Storing office supplies Storing chemical substances for shop-floor Tools and components	Small trolley Range of metal shelving & racks	1

Checklist 5: Movement of goods through the business

Area on site plan	What happens at this stage?	Who deals with it?
Stage 1: Arrival		
Stage 2: Process		
Stage 3: Process		
Stage 4: Completion or finishing		
Stage 5: Delivery		

3 Identify hazards

Safety hazards

Hazard = something with the potential to cause harm or injury. It is not about whether you think it actually will cause such harm, but that you are aware that it exists as a potential source. We shall look at how likely it is when we assess risks.

People tend to be more aware of the major safety hazards associated with their trade or industry sector rather than health or even fire hazards. Safety hazards are often more visible than things that can harm your health, so it is easier to start by spotting them. It doesn't matter how you record your findings, but it is useful to refer to the flowchart and site plans to draw up your list of hazards. Identify safety hazards associated with the following activities or processes if they apply to your workplace. Typical hazards are followed by a list of things to look for.

Vehicles

▶ Being run over by the vehicle as it is moving or reversing

▶ The driver's view in the mirror being restricted.

▶ Being crushed, either behind or at the side of the vehicle.

▶ Vehicles overturning where the ground is not firm or is pitted.

Look for:

▷ Limited space allowed for vehicles to turn or manouvre.

▷ Objects that restrict the view of vehicles as they move about the site.

▷ No pedestrian and vehicle separation, no clear pedestrian crossings.

▷ The way people drive on site – are they trained and competent?

Machinery

▶ Moving parts of machinery or equipment exposed.

▶ Clothing trapped in the machine.

▶ Hair or jewellery entangled.

▶ Being hit by moving parts of the machine.

▶ Materials/objects thrown out by the machine (projectiles).

- ▶ Bands or cords that move quickly have the potential to break and snake out, causing a whipping action.
- ▶ Abrasive and rough surfaces that can cause burns.
- ▶ Fast-spin machines such as centrifuges or dryers.

Look for:
- ▷ Guards and handrails broken or missing.
- ▷ Parts of machine modified to cut-out safety devices.
- ▷ Temporary repairs.
- ▷ Records of previous accidents/incidents/damage/near-misses using particular equipment or machinery.

Sharp tools and objects

- ▶ Machines for chopping, cutting, mincing, and shredding.
- ▶ Use of knives and blades – food preparation, opening boxes, cutting materials such as carpet or floorcovering.
- ▶ Office environments – use of guillotines, sharp edges of paper; (they may not be significant hazards, but should be recognised).
- ▶ Sharp instruments, e.g. hand drills, hand-held equipment.
- ▶ Needles, surgical instruments.

Look for:
- ▷ The way machines are used, state of repair of equipment.
- ▷ Use and storage of knives and blades.
- ▷ Small instruments and portable equipment.
- ▷ Where/how needles and other 'sharps' are disposed of.

Heat

- ▶ Burns and scalds when working with heated objects or materials.
- ▶ Use of cookers/ovens in catering or kilns in craft activities.
- ▶ Use of glass-washing machines (in pubs and hotels for instance).
- ▶ Using a photocopier – if paper is jammed, internal parts can be hot when the machine is opened.
- ▶ Welding machines, sparks flying and heat from the process itself.
- ▶ Extreme cold can potentially cause burns and frostbite damage.

Look for: ▷ Areas with fans or cooling systems.

▷ Temperature-controlled equipment and machinery.

▷ Warning signs about wearing correct protective clothing.

Electricity

▶ Death from electric shock if in contact with the electrical supply.

▶ Falls from heights after receiving a shock.

▶ Burns – internal and external damage.

▶ Unconsciousness, heart attack.

Look for: ▷ Large pieces of equipment and machinery powered by electricity.

▷ Hand-held electrical equipment.

▷ Portable elecetrical equipment that is regularly plugged and un-plugged from sockets.

▷ Worn cables, casings, repairs with tape, loose connections.

▷ Damage, signs of burning on plug sockets.

▷ Anywhere where extension cables are used.

▷ Overloaded or broken sockets.

▷ Trailing cables across busy pedestrian traffic routes.

▷ Rest areas and places where people make tea and coffee.

▷ Water near where electrical equipment is used or plugged in.

Working at heights

▶ Falls from height when using ladders, steps or scaffolding.

▶ Dropping objects from height.

▶ Using electrical equipment when working at height (see above).

▶ Accessing fragile surfaces (including glass or asbestos).

Look for: ▷ Activities that require someone working more than two metres above the ground (this could be inside a container or in a pit).

▷ Use of steps, ladders or scaffold.

▷ People climbing on chairs, cupboards, etc. instead of stepladders.

▷ Warehouse and stores activities.

▷ Areas on the site plan with glass or asbestos roof.

▷ remember to include maintenance activities.

Confined spaces

This is usually associated with people who have to work inside tank bodies, in underground workings or cellars in pubs and licensed premises, but could also include loft or other cavity areas in construction.

▶ Limited access, movement and breathing facilities.

▶ Sitting or lying in cramped areas with little room to manouvre themselves or equipment.

▶ Using welding or blow-torch equipment inside vehicles, vessels or other containers.

Look for:

▷ Cramped work areas with little head-room.

▷ Vehicles, vessels that need someone to work from the inside.

▷ Equipment in use, particularly things that produce heat or fumes.

▷ Formal safe systems of work, or time limits for certain tasks.

Slips, trips and falls

▶ Shiny, smooth floor surfaces.

▶ Water, oil, grease, powders or dusts on floor surfaces.

▶ Waste materials and scrap lying around the floor.

▶ Changes of floor level, steps and stairs.

What needs recording?

Legislation does not require you to write down the results of your assessment of hazards and risks unless you employ five people or more. Moreover, it says you must record the results of 'significant' findings, rather than every minor detail about every activity in your business that could possibly result in harm. It does NOT require you to carry out a risk assessment on the use of Tippex correction fluid!

Look for:
- ▷ Obstructions in passageways, fire exit routes and on stairs.
- ▷ Loose, rough, or worn edges of carpet and other floor coverings.
- ▷ Cables or air lines across pedestrian routes.
- ▷ Spillages or build-up of grease/dirt on floor surfaces.
- ▷ Lighting on stairs, in passageways, near exits.

Lifting and carrying

- ▶ Back and upper body injuries from incorrect lifting techniques.
- ▶ Twisting or bending when moving loads.
- ▶ Strains and sprains.
- ▶ Crush injuries or broken limbs.
- ▶ Trips and falls if load too heavy or awkward shape.
- ▶ Cuts from sharp edges in packaging or objects.
- ▶ Same hazards associated with lifting people and animals.

Look for:
- ▷ Size and shape of loads.
- ▷ Use of manual and mechanical means to lift or carry things.

I'm sorry, ma'am, but I can't help. Your bag is 5g over the health and safety limit.

> The weight in relation to other elements (for example, weight combined with action of silver-service waitress/waiter as they support server on outstretched arm).

> People moving awkwardly once they have lifted the object.

> Storage areas, height of shelving.

> Tasks involving lifting people or animals.

Repetitive strain injuries

▶ Regularly repeated movement putting a strain on joints.

▶ Fast, repetitive and often small movements, for example when using of computer keyboards.

Look for:

> Areas where workers twist in their seat to perform parts of the task.

> Keyboard operators.

> Small movements associated with manual dexterity of the hands.

> Tasks that are repeated in the same manner throughout the shift.

> Some vibrating/drilling machines can cause problems when used for any length of time.

Personal safety

▶ Working with the public and the threat of personal violence.

▶ Working alone, especially when travelling between sites.

▶ Robbery and violence when the person is transporting money or valuables on behalf of the firm.

▶ Potential injury when working with animals.

Look for:

> Staff who open up or lock up premises (often on their own).

> Front-line staff who work directly with the customer.

> Staff who travel regularly between sites, often out of normal office hours.

> Staff who deliver/collect money or valuables for the company.

> Activities that involve sick people or animals who may be under emotional strain.

Travel

▶ Setting timescales for Sales or Delivery staff that are impossible to meet except by breaking the law and speed limits.

▶ Heavy workload leading to tiredness and potential mistakes.

▶ Dealing with accident and emergency situations when driving.

▶ Distance to move deliveries if parking restrictions in towns.

Chemicals and gases

Chemicals

▶ Burns to the skin.

▶ Damage to internal organs from breathing in gases.

▶ Nausea, dizziness, loss of consciousness from inhaling/ingesting chemical substances.

Look for:

▷ Evidence of substances transferred from one container to another.

▷ Unidentified/ unlabelled substances stored and used.

▷ Open containers around work areas.

▷ Chemicals storage cupboards not closed and locked.

Use of compressed air or LPG

Typical hazards relate to explosion and fire, and the source of oxygen in the event of a fire. Compressed air can also be a hazard if used incorrectly.

Look for:

▷ Where these products are used and stored.

▷ Mobile supplies of LPG.

▷ Trailing compressed air lines.

▷ Horseplay amongst staff using these products.

 ## Workplace-specific hazards

There may be other activities or processes specific to your workplace that are associated with injuries – or near misses –so include these as well.

40

Health hazards

As with safety hazards, there are many different ways you can define 'health hazards', but from a practical point of view the following list of headings should cover the most common types. It is often much more difficult to see how far the way you work might threaten or damage your health, particularly when some situations result in damage only after a very long latency period – exposure to asbestos fibres, for example.

Physical working conditions

> See also safety hazards as these are often combined in a work task.

Noise levels

Noise is unwanted sound. It can cause hearing loss, even at fairly low levels, and is very debilitating for those concerned. What is more, it often takes place over a long period of time. People do get used to background noise, so you must check levels where people regularly have to shout to each other to be heard.

▶ Damage caused by long-term exposure to high levels of noise, or regular short-term blasts of noise over a working day.

▶ Constant repetition of certain types of noise, leading to distress or inability to concentrate.

▶ Short-term or long-term hearing loss, possibly leading to premature deafness.

▶ Tinnitus – a constant whining or ringing noise inside the ear.

Look for:

▷ Physical surroundings that can make sound levels worse, e.g. outer cabinet walls vibrating with sound rather than absorbing it.

▷ Situations where staff are required to use telephone headsets for long periods such as call centre facilities.

▷ Areas of workplace where noise levels are higher than other areas.

▷ Length of exposure to noise during the working day.

▷ Loud music playing, or sound with a strong underlying base beat.

▷ Complaints and signs of stress in workers exposed to noise.

Noise pollution is a broader problem. You may need to consider:

Are some of the processes very loud, particularly from outside the works?

Do they take place outside normal weekday business hours 0900-1700?

Have they increased as the scale of operations or type of machinery has changed?

Lighting levels

▶ Poor or inappropriate lighting can lead to headaches, eye-strain, pains in back or neck muscles.

▶ People may also show symptoms of stress, depression or fatigue.

▶ For both close and distance work, the amount of natural light is very important.

Look for:

▷ Areas where lighting causes shadows or glare on computer screens and other equipment.

▷ Lighting levels in areas such as stairs, lobbies and storage places.

▷ The type of light makes a difference to how comfortable it is to work – note where low wattage, fluorescent or daylight bulbs are used.

▷ Broken light fittings or missing bulbs.

Temperature levels

◆ Extremes of heat or cold (including changes in work temperatures depending to the season).

◆ Ventilation and humidity levels.

◆ Lower levels of dexterity and concentration if temperature not appropriate.

> There is a statutory minimum work temperature in many situations.

◆ Depending on the type of work being carried out, there may be difficulty in breathing normally, and potential loss of consciousness.

Look for:

▷ People working in chill houses or freezers for long periods of time.

▷ People working inside and outside in same shift, and whether suitable clothing is available.

▷ Cold spots or draughty areas.

▷ Window areas where sunlight causes glare or concentrates heat.

Air quality

♦ Level of visible dust particles in the air.

♦ Tiny particles that are virtually invisible to the eye may be even more hazardous and just appear as clouds of 'mist'.

♦ Exhaust fumes from vehicles in work area.

♦ Poor air quality may lead to fairly minor coughing, nausea or eye irritation.

♦ It may also have an impact on breathing/respiratory actions, and cause drowsiness or symptoms similar to being intoxicated.

Look for:

▷ Existing extraction or ventilation systems are adequate and working, whether local or general systems.

▷ Extraction and ventilation systems that emit exhaust fumes.

▷ The volume of extraction and how hazardous these exhaust fumes might be to surrounding areas and the environment.

▷ Symptoms of poor air quality (as above) or areas where people have asked for better ventilation.

▷ Areas where people work in confined spaces.

▷ Dust or other particles layered on machinery and work areas.

▷ Dust particles clogging ventilation outlets.

 These last three categories of physical working conditions (light, temperature and air) can have a negative impact on morale and motivation, which may result in dissatisfaction with the job and therefore loss of concentration and commitment.

Computers and visual display units (VDUs)

Users of computers/VDUs should take regular breaks from looking at the screen – they do not have to leave the workstation, but they should vary the activity.

♦ Upper body, neck and back pain from incorrect posture or insufficient breaks from the work.

♦ Pain in wrists and fingers from repetitive, small movements on keyboard.

- Eye damage from use of VDU and glare on screen (from lights or sun).

- Potential for minute levels of radiation from screens (not fully proven).

Look for:
  ▷ Where the VDUs or screens are positioned in relation to keyboards and seating.

  ▷ Workstations that can be adjusted to suit the individual user – height of screen, chair height, bend of elbows as arms rest on table.

  ▷ Use of wrist rests for keyboard use.

  ▷ Lighting is appropriate to avoid screen glare.

  ▷ Workload and time available for regular rest breaks.

Micro-organisms and airborne contaminants

If your business is in food preparation, you will already be registered with the Local Authority and be following the detailed requirements of HACCP (Hazard Analysis and Control of Critical Points).

- Food poisoning/illnesses from contaminated food preparation areas, including work and floor surfaces, temperatures in fridges, food reheating facilities, washing facilities.

- Airborne contagious diseases carried by clients, customers, other staff, or in areas where you are working with animals.

- Specific contaminants such as those associated with blood products (if you work with these you will already be aware of the hazards).

- Inappropriate disposal of products in skips or other refuse collection facilities.

Disposal issues

Disposal of products and objects associated with micro-organisms or airborne contagious disease is also an environmental issue. Appropriate systems must be in place to ensure proper isolation and labelling of such waste, and correct disposal and collection procedures are followed. If unsure of the level of contaminants, contact the local environmental health office for guidance.

Look for:
- ▷ Areas where food is prepared, stored or served.
- ▷ Information and hazard data sheets about the products being used.
- ▷ Notices and information about procedures and protective clothing or equipment required.
- ▷ Waste and rubbish collection facilities.

Radiation

This is a very specific source of hazard that you should already be aware of if it is an issue in your industry sector.

- ◆ Low-dosage radiation is potentially a hazard to female workers who are (or could be) pregnant or nursing mothers.
- ◆ Exposure at low levels and potential impact on the individual's fertility levels.
- ◆ Environmental damage by emissions into the atmosphere.

Look for:
- ▷ Records of maintenance of equipment that emits any radiation.
- ▷ Health monitoring systems in place.
- ▷ Access to the hazardous equipment or process by staff.
- ▷ Procedures for disposal of potentially contaminated waste products.

Use of chemical and other substances

Hazardous substances are those that have the potential to cause harm or injury when used, stored or disposed of. The Control of Substances Hazardous to Health (COSHH) regulations outline the actions you must take to make sure people are safe from harm when handling or working with them.

Substances can be liquid, gas, fumes or dust. They can be absorbed through direct contact with the skin, swallowing, breathing, or through other means such as puncture wounds.

If you use substances such as solvents, adhesives, inks, dyes or mineral oils, you should already have a system in place for making sure all staff know about the hazards associated with using them. Any chemicals that have some form of 'danger' sign on the container, are likely to have a hazard data sheet that the manufacturer has produced. They broadly follow the same pattern in that they tell you exactly what the hazard is, the harm it may cause, correct storage and handling procedures and protection for users, and relevant treatment in the event of mishandling.

◆ Eczema or dermatitis-type skin conditions, which are often extremely debilitating and usually long-term or recurrent.

◆ Some chemicals can act as 'sensitisers' to severe effects in the future if an individual comes into contact with the substance again.

◆ Some are carcinogenic (i.e. with the potential to cause cancer).

Look for:

▷ Environmentally-friendly methods for use, storage and disposal.

▷ Where substances are stored, inside or outside the buildings, and whether they are in secure appropriate cupboards or containers.

▷ Evidence of leakage into ground or watercourses.

▷ How waste products are disposed of.

▷ How contaminated materials are disposed of; where empty containers are stored for disposal (still with traces of chemicals inside).

 There are many bleach-based or otherwise hazardous substances used in hairdressing, and a wide range of chemicals used in agriculture.

Use of materials and fibres

Many of these dusts are potentially cancer-forming and most can lead to respiratory, digestive or skin diseases.

◆ Production or storage areas where dusts and fibres can escape into the air.

◆ Production of agricultural preparations and fertilisers.

◆ Wood dusts from sawing/sanding.

◆ Cement and similar products in construction.

◆ Flour dust in bakery areas.

◆ Asbestos fibres, found in older premises, lagging for heating systems, corrugated asbestos-cement roof panels.

Look for:	▷	Evidence of dust on surfaces in work areas.
	▷	Equipment with in-built or local ventilation systems.
	▷	Use of materials that produce dust or fibres when they are processed.
	▷	Possible leakage.
	▷	Method of disposal of such materials.

Smoking

Smoking will be banned in public and work places in the UK during 2007, but if you visit clients in their own home, this may still be a potential hazard to consider. (The question of workers in the leisure industry, or carers in sheltered accommodation for the elderly has yet to be resolved.)

- ◆ Serious damage to lung and throat tissue.
- ◆ Irritation and discomfort experienced by non-smokers.

Look for:

▷ Areas where smoking is specifically restricted or allowed, and the ventilation systems in place.

▷ The stated company policy for smokers and non-smokers in your business. (see page 88). You need to consider the impact of smoke on non-smokers, and the atmospheric conditions in work and rest areas. This is a difficult issue as there may be a question about how far you can protect workers in, for example, the leisure or care industry sectors (but note the new ban on smoking in public places).

Manual handling

Manual handling relates to lifting, pushing, pulling, holding and gripping objects, materials, animals or people.

- ▶ Twisting movements, or situations that require more than one handling movement at the same time, such as lifting and pushing a storage box onto a high shelf.
- ▶ Repetition of small movements can be damaging over time.

Look for:

▷ Production process that relies on twisting, repetitive movements.

▷ A computer or checkout system that relies on speed for its effectiveness.

Stress and work organisation

Evidence suggests that the way work is organised can have a significant impact on how stress is handled. It is extremely difficult to be precise about causes of stress, as people react differently to the same situations. However, you have a duty to protect workers' health. While the owner of a business may see stress differently from workers, it must be accepted that they are not paid to take on the same responsibilities as the owner!

◆ Feelings of not being able to cope effectively with a situation.

◆ Being set unrealistic targets, with insufficient equipment or materials to complete the job properly within the tight deadline set.

◆ Insufficient training or chance to learn the skills properly.

◆ Few rest breaks during or between shifts, leading to tiredness and lack of concentration.

◆ Bullying or violence at work, either internally or in contact with customers, can be a significant factor in the levels of well-being experienced by staff.

Look for:

▷ Shift patterns worked, schedules and targets set.

▷ Whether set rest periods are taken.

▷ Sickness absence levels and lack of motivation amongst staff.

There may be other potentially hazardous situations that you can identify in your business, and as we said previously, using the Site plans should ensure that you have considered all the relevant areas of the firm. Note all the results on Checklist 10, numbering each hazard as you go along so that you can refer to it more easily on the next two Checklists to assess the Risks and identify the Controls.

Fire is a higher risk

Recent changes to the law in the UK mean that even if you only employ one person, you must carry out a fire risk assessment in the same way that you assess health and safety risks. Read on...

Fire hazards

While most people are familiar with health and safety hazards, it is sadly the case that unless you have witnessed the speed and destructive power of a fire at first hand, you are unlikely to be fully aware of what we mean by fire hazards. The local fire authority is always willing to offer advice about your own circumstances, and although you might need to call on some professional assistance at some time, the majority of your fire risk assessment can be carried out by you and your workers.

If you already have a fire certificate (these no longer have any legal status) or other form of approval from the fire authority, you will still need to do a risk assessment.

The process is the same as the one we have followed so far. Start with your site plans, as much of the fire risk assessment can be carried out by reference to these plans. If there are areas of shared ownership, or multiple use of buildings, you must notify other people of your findings.

A few points worth remembering before we start to identify fire hazards.

! Smoke from a fire rises to the ceiling, gets trapped there, then spreads wherever it can.

! It quickly spreads to other parts of the building through any holes or gaps.

! The smoke can be extremely toxic depending on what materials are burning.

! Heat from the fire – not only flames – can cause materials to ignite or explode.

! Flames can leap across to other buildings or structures.

! Fire and smoke will spread rapidly in open-plan areas, roof cavities, corridors and stair wells.

The hazards associated with fire are the three elements it needs in order to burn – sometimes referred to as the **fire triangle** – which are:

◆ A source of **ignition**, like a spark, naked flame or hot surface.

◆ **Fuel** to keep it going such as flammable gases and liquids, or other flammable materials.

◆ **Oxygen**, which is of course present in the air but may also come from chemical substances or pressurised containers.

The Fire Triangle

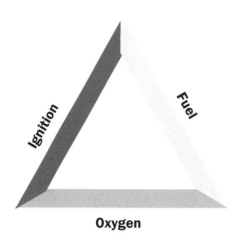

Oxygen

To identify fire hazards, use the following checklist and a further copy of the site plan to identify:

◆ Internal and external areas where fire hazards may exist.

◆ Firefighting equipment and alarm systems that are in place.

◆ Escape routes.

◆ Areas where action is required to reduce risks to people.

Checklist 6: Fire hazards on site

Area of hazard identified	Sources of ignition?	Sources of fuel?	Sources of oxygen?	How many people?	Controls identified?

Use this as a summary list when identifying these details on plan (extra rows can be added).

Sources of ignition

Go over a site plan, showing outside areas as well as internal features, and identify with a red 'I' where you find potential sources of heat or ignition. It is worth looking out for places where you know fires have previously taken place or been avoided due to someone's quick actions.

Typical ignition sources include:

▶ Cigarettes, matches and lighters.

▶ Heaters using gas, electricity or oil as a fuel.

▶ Naked flames, pilot lights, cookers, etc.

▶ Welding or grinding machinery, or processes which produce sparks.

▶ Lights or other smaller pieces of equipment where surfaces get hot.

▶ Faulty electrical equipment or areas of high static electricity.

Fuel sources

These include anything that burns fairly easily, especially where it is used or stored in large quantities – not just sources that are likely to start a fire, but also the fuel that could feed it and keep it going. Using the site plan, identify with a red 'F' the potential sources of fuel. Do not forget to include waste disposal areas outside the buildings too.

Typical fuel sources include:

▶ Wood, paper, cardboard and packaging.

▶ Organic materials such as flour, cereal and animal feed.

▶ Furniture and shelving or other fittings.

▶ Furnishings and fabrics or similar fibres.

▶ Foam, polystyrene, polyurethane or similar products, whether they are part of your production process or part of the building structure.

▶ Chemicals and solvents, especially petrol or spirit-based products.

▶ Paint, varnish, adhesive products.

▶ Gases such as LPG and acetylene (generally found in cylinders).

Look for: ▷ Processes which release dusts and fibres into the air.

> How dense fibres are and how far they float into the air.

> The way your building is constructed and laid out internally, including stairwells, ceiling cavities, storage areas, rarely-used cupboards.

If you are uncertain about these, contact the local fire authority for advice.

Sources of oxygen

Obviously, we need oxygen in the air we breathe, so unless your workplace is in a hostile environment (such as underwater or underground) this source will be present in sufficient quantities to fuel a fire. Add details to your site plan using red 'O' to indicate sources such as the following:

Typical hazards include:

♦ The ventilation system will ensure oxygen is moving freely around the building and may even add more.

♦ A clear air-flow route around the room/building might increase the likelihood that a fire will keep burning.

♦ Processes you carry out might involve using pressurised containers, air or oxygen cylinders that could add to the spread of a fire.

♦ Some chemicals you use can act as oxidising agents (you should already know which ones these are as the details should be included on the labels/manufacturers' instructions for use and storage).

♦ External windows and doors that open, or are regularly propped open, can provide additional oxygen to the room or building.

Look for:

> Areas that might be particularly vulnerable to arson attack, and to the careless disposal of cigarettes.

> Where pressurised containers/oxygen are stored and used.

> Shutting-down facilities for ventilation systems.

> Skips and waste containers where materials that are individually safe are mixed with other elements of the fire triangle.

Fires can start in unexpected places

Few people realise the potential for a fire to start inside a bin of waste rags soaked in inks or solvents, seemingly without a source of ignition being added.

4 Controlling risks

Risk assessment

Risk assessment is the process of identifying those hazards with potential to cause harm or injury, deciding who could be harmed and the type and severity of harm that might occur, then assessing the likelihood that this will happen.

The process goes further, considering suitable controls to reduce risks as far as you can, taking action to put new controls in place if existing ones are missing or inadequate. You must then monitor the impact of these actions, regularly reviewing the system to make sure it is still relevant.

There are so many different methods available to help you assess the health and safety risks in your workplace, that it is no wonder people become confused! The process is not intended to be a complicated, academic exercise that can only be carried out by a specialist, but a logical approach to assess the risk that a hazard will result in harm or injury.

There may be areas where technical or specialist help is needed, when assessing levels of noise or density of particles in the air for instance, but the bulk of the risk assessment can be carried out by you.

Having produced a comprehensive list of potential hazards in your workplace, you should now be able to take this a step further and consider the potential risks to people, based on:

◆   Who could be harmed.

◆   The severity of that harm.

◆   The likelihood that it will occur.

You don't have to give a numerical value to these evaluations, such as a rating of 1–10, but can make a judgement based on criteria such as High, Medium, Low.

Using the list of activities carried out in each area and the potential hazards identified, use the following headings to assess the risks.

Who could be harmed?

For each hazard, note:

◆ Which individual workers are in direct contact with it.

◆ Whether these people are exposed to the hazard most of the working shift, occasionally during the shift, on odd occasions, or perhaps once a year when maintenance is carried out.

◆ Other people who could be harmed, such as customers or visitors, cleaning contractors or businesses you share the premises with.

◆ Anyone who may *potentially* be more prone to the effects of the hazard, or less able to deal with situations or processes.

Vulnerable groups

Some groups of people may be more vulnerable to a particular hazard, e.g.

❖ Young people under the age of 18 years old, whose lack of experience and expertise may increase the likelihood that injury or harm will occur.

❖ Older workers who may be extremely competent but who sometimes develop novel shortcuts to processes over time!

❖ Potentially at greater risk are nursing or pregnant women, who should be identified in your risk assessments.

Statistics show that men up to 25 are most likely to experience accidents in the workplace, though not generally very severe ones: men aged 50+ are less likely to have an accident, but when they do it is likely to result in death or a major injury.

Severity of harm

This is about the potential for harm or injury associated with each of the hazards. It is a very subjective activity and people differ widely in how they define severity of harm. However, you should be able to make a fair and reasonable judgement based on your own experience in the business.

It will help to refer to accident or sickness records to remind you of the sort of injury that might occur, plus any manufacturers' guidance or information notes. Think about the type of injury possible so that you can decide the level of severity.

Severity ratings

The following headings illustrate how you might decide a severity rating for each of the hazards you have identified.

♦ **Low or slightly harmful**, e.g. minor cuts and bruises or superficial injuries that require First Aid treatment.

♦ **Medium or harmful**, e.g. serious sprains or minor fractures, burns or concussion that result in lost time or hospital visits.

♦ **High or extremely harmful**, e.g. major injuries, fractures, amputations and of course, death.

Likelihood of harm or injury

Based on the range of activities and hazards identified, plus your evaluation of what harm or injury is likely to occur and who is most likely to be affected, consider what the risk is that something WILL occur.

You could use the following criteria to assess the likelihood of harm:

♦ **High** – if the activity occurs regularly, and it is already seen as a problem by workers or others.

♦ **Medium** – something that happens perhaps once a month rather than daily or weekly.

♦ **Low** – very irregular contact, perhaps for very short amounts of time in any given period, or a highly-controlled activity with many safeguards already in place.

It may be a pretty depressing list by this time, with every aspect of your work potentially very hazardous! However, the point is that there are many ways to eliminate, reduce or control these risks. Some may already be in place, and some will require very little additional action.

More people x more time = more likely

The higher number of people exposed to a hazard, and longer the exposure time, the more likelihood that some harm or injury will occur.

Priorities for further action

You cannot deal with everything at the same time, and some risks will be more significant than others or will need quite urgent attention.

As the law requires you to record the results of 'significant' findings of risk assessments, there needs to be some form of rating system in place to help you decide what is significant or not.

The risk table below shows one way to consider each hazard against the two criteria:

◆ The severity of potential harm

◆ The likelihood that it will occur.

Risk table 1: Assessing the risk

	Slightly harmful	Harmful	Extremely harmful
Highly unlikely	TRIVIAL RISK 1	2	3
Likely	2	3	4
Very Likely	3	4	URGENT ACTION REQUIRED – INTOLERABLE RISK 5

The numbers represent a range from:

1 = Trivial, or acceptable level of residual risk.

5 = Intolerable/urgent action required

If you have several activities appearing in the 'Very likely/Extremely harmful' sector, with a rating of 4–5, then clearly urgent action is needed.

While you may decide that little or no action is required to reduce the risks further at the 'Highly unlikely/Low harm' point (sometimes referred to as the 'trivial risk' point), this does not mean that you should just ignore your findings and expect people to accept the inherent risk without providing any controls at all.

Existing controls

We have already mentioned controls that exist to safeguard workers or other people, and to reduce risk of injury or harm. While it is generally easy to see physical guards and controls, especially in production or manufacturing areas, there are many other forms of control which you will already have in place.

The assessment of risk carried out so far demonstrates that you:

◆ Are fully aware of what happens in your organisation.

◆ Know how work progresses through the system.

◆ Know what the main activities are in each area and who does what.

You have also assessed the potential risks to people of injury or harm, and decided which elements of risk need further consideration.

Before you can decide the actions needed to reduce risks, it is important to look at existing controls, identify any gaps and decide where new controls need to be introduced.

Order of actions to establish effective controls

1 Elimination

2 Substitution

3 Restricting access

4 Guards and physical controls

5 Procedures

6 Training and supervision

7 Personal protective equipment (PPE).

We'll leave elimination and substitution to the side while we look at the types of controls that we can use.

Types of control

Restricted access

Access to certain areas, machines or substances is restricted to control the hazard, through:

- Security code locks on access doors.
- Only trained personnel allowed to carry out tasks, e.g. driving a fork-lift truck.
- Designated hard-hat/hearing defender/protective clothing areas.
- Notices to warn people they may be approaching restricted or hazardous areas.
- Restricted access to personnel already identified as more susceptible to the hazards.

Guards and physical controls

There are many forms of physical controls, and it will depend on the type of industry you are in, but the following may already exist:

- Guard rails and covers for machinery or equipment when in use.
- Fail-safe systems to cut off power to machines in an emergency.
- Stop buttons or mats.
- Adequate alarm systems to warn users or passers by that some hazard exists, e.g. when vehicles are reversing.
- Local or general exhaust and ventilation systems which are adequate and appropriate for the conditions.
- The use of PPE by individuals in certain areas on the site, or when carrying out specific tasks.
- Muffling on machinery casings to reduce vibration and noise.
- Meters and other recording systems that are regularly checked and maintained, with in-built alarms to warn of unsafe levels.
- Closed containers for moving or storing hazardous substances.

Procedures

Procedures should be established to reduce risks and ensure tasks are carried out safely. These might include:

- Regular checks to ensure good standards are maintained.
- Specified safe procedures for carrying out tasks.
- Formal 'safe system of work' procedures which rely on authorised personnel taking responsibility for ensuring systems are followed correctly, particular hazardous activities, e.g. when machines are turned off for maintenance, or roof work is being carried out.
- Regular programme of testing machinery or equipment, and recording results – essential for pressure equipment, lifting gear.
- Regular visual checks and testing of portable electrical equipment.
- Regular checks before the use of ladders, scaffolding, etc.
- Proper use of hazard data sheets from suppliers.
- Regular programme of maintenance and oiling working parts of machinery, to reduce noise.
- Organisation of work for VDU users, to ensure adequate rest periods and breaks from using the screen; provision of eye tests, and spectacles where necessary.
- Good housekeeping and cleaning regimes maintained.
- Designated 'Smoking' and 'No Smoking' areas.
- Appropriate decontamination procedures and adequate washing/ toilet facilities.
- Adequate breaks to reduce stress or discomfort, and suitable rest areas.
- First aid and other training to ensure proper help in emergency situations, e.g. breathing difficulties or spillages of contaminants.
- Regular checks on dust, noise, temperature and contaminant levels in relevant areas.
- Regular hearing tests to monitor any increase in hearing loss over time.
- Records of monitoring health of staff exposed to potential health hazards such as air contaminants, radiation, or micro-organisms.

Training and supervision

Training staff to ensure they know how to carry out work safely is an effective control, as is proper supervision to make sure everyone follows the rules. Various things can come under this heading, including:

- Training and qualifications in specific areas, e.g. manual handling; fork lift truck driving; welding; use of hazardous substances.
- In-house training programmes at induction or on use of particular machines.
- Training to handle or work with specified processes.
- Training in storage, handling and/or disposal of very hazardous substances.
- Training in how to handle potentially violent situations, including self defence.
- Adequate training for lone workers who may be particularly vulnerable.
- Training in proper use and care of PPE.
- Direct supervision where hazardous activities take place.
- Supervision to ensure PPE is worn where deemed necessary.

Personal protective equipment (PPE)

When other methods of control cannot be used to reduce the risks further, the last option may be protective equipment for the individual worker. This includes things such as:

- Protective clothing such as overalls; appropriate gloves; thermal wear; hats; hairnets.
- Hard hats; toe-protection footwear.
- Specialist wear such as rubber-soled footwear where there is a danger of electric shock.
- Goggles; hard-lens spectacles.
- Chainmail aprons or gloves; reinforced wear (such as that containing Kevlar) for forestry work.
- Harnesses for working at height or in confined spaces.

- Personal alarms.

- Disposable single-use protective wear.

- Ear plugs and ear defenders.

- Spectacles for use with VDUs or other equipment.

- Masks that cover nose and mouth, with range of appropriate types of filter pads to fit.

- More complex breathing apparatus that ensures a flow of breathable air and covers more of the face or head.

- Hands-free telephone equipment.

- Wrist or body supports for lifting activities.

Control measures needed

When deciding what actions are needed to reduce risks to workers, you should consider the following list of controls in this order.

1 Elimination

Clearly the best way to protect someone from potential injury or harm is to remove the cause – that is, the hazard itself. So, for example, if a machine presents a particular hazard, then scrapping it altogether may be the most sensible option you can take. Risks associated with using certain types of materials or processes, may be significant enough to consider alternatives or review future investment and purchasing plans.

2 Substitution

Elimination of the source of the harm may not be feasible. It might be more sensible to consider substituting materials, machines or equipment with less-hazardous versions. For example, safer tools than short-blade hand-held knives can be used to open cartons or boxes. Materials may be available in different formats or strengths to safeguard the user.

Don't forget, you will need to reassess the risks when a substitution is made, to ensure you have not introduced some new hazard.

Good for the environment and good for your business

As consumers and manufacturers become more aware of environmental issues related to use and disposal of materials, substituting more eco-friendly materials or substances could give commercial as well as safety benefits to your business.

Contact your suppliers for further information on what or how you can substitute products.

3 Restricting access to the hazard

If you cannot remove the hazard, another option is to remove people from contact with it. Enclose or screen-off a machine or process that presents significant risks to the user or passer-by. Potential injury while in contact with the public in sensitive situations may be more difficult, particularly if a physical barrier is inappropriate to the service being provided. In some government offices, for instance, there are permanent security guards on hand if required.

Locked cages and cabinets for storing some materials may be a simple but effective option, and could fit with the controls needed for fire risks. Access can be controlled by a designated key holder or nominated person per shift. Check if there is specific guidance, or best practice advice, available from within your industry sector.

4 Physical guards and controls

Some equipment and machinery comes from the manufacturer complete with in-built physical controls or guards. Unfortunately, we all know how inventive workers can be when trying to by-pass these controls! The company is responsible for making sure adequate guards or controls are:

◆   in place;

◆   in working order;

◆   appropriate for what they are guarding against;

◆   used correctly at all times.

It is more difficult to install new guarding systems to old machines, but not impossible given new developments in technology. Contact manufacturers and suppliers for further information as the first stage of your Action Plan.

There are physical guards that can protect people from noise, radiation, and other contaminants. These may rely on appropriate containers being identified and used correctly, but they also rely on people being trained and supervised properly.

5 Procedures

Working procedures must be appropriate and safe for those following them. They must also recognise the needs of specific groups of workers, such as young workers or people with disabilities that restrict activities.

Consider shift or work patterns, rest periods, and any repetitive tasks that make up the job. Don't forget that the schedules set for drivers should allow for any restrictive access times for commercial vehicles, the dangers of using mobile phones, and the restrictions on driving times imposed by tracking devices.

6 Training and supervision

This is not a substitute for having appropriate controls in place, but is a vital element in reducing risks and the likelihood that accidents will occur. It may be difficult if you have a rapid turnover of staff, or regularly use temporary or contract workers. However, it does not necessarily involve sending people off-site for training. Some manufacturers provide training on the use of their products, and you will need to find out what is available locally to establish a training plan for staff.

If new processes or procedures are introduced, people will need to know what they are and will need to be adequately supervised until they are familiar with them. You must ensure that people are adequately trained and supervised, so that they:

♦ Are aware of the hazards associated with the tasks.

♦ Know the correct procedures to follow.

♦ Understand why they must follow them in this way.

♦ Can recognise early enough when things are not going well.

It is not good enough to tell them to read a manual to find out how to work some equipment or machinery. You are responsible for making sure they do know and understand how to perform tasks safely.

7 Personal protective equipment

This is the last line of defence to protect workers, and should only be considered when other forms of protection or control are not feasible in the circumstances. Many firms see this as the easiest way to control the hazards, and sometimes the cheapest, but it should only be used to offer very specific protection to an individual who cannot be fully protected by other means. Clearly, there are some circumstances where it is appropriate, using breathing apparatus for instance when other controls over the atmosphere are not possible. Metal link aprons and gloves are used in the butchery trade as the use of knives and cleavers cannot easily be eliminated or substituted!

There are many forms of PPE available, and manufacturers are happy to provide help and guidance. The main points to consider are:

- The specific hazard that is being protected against.

- Whether the suggested PPE is appropriate for this hazard.

- That people know and understand how to use PPE correctly.

- That it is kept clean, maintained properly and replaced at suitable intervals.

- That it fits correctly, especially if more than one form of PPE is used at a time (for example, goggles and breathing mask).

- That it is not a substitute for other forms of control.

Identifiying the hazard is just the start

This section is intended to help you move a step further than just spotting hazards and identifying potential risks to workers and others. While both those steps are a valuable starting point, you have to then take some action to make sure that if they cannot be eliminated, residual risks are controlled adequately.

5 Fire risks

Who is at risk?

Fire risks are much more closely tied to location than to specific activities. The potential for harm or injury to an occasional visitor on site is relatively low, but they will be at greater risk from fire than someone who is familiar with the site. You will need to give greater consideration to the potential risks to customers, contractors, and even unauthorised visitors who may be on site if a fire occurs. An assessment of the risks must also consider other businesses that share the premises with you, and areas of communal or joint use, such as entrance halls, stair-wells, rubbish disposal points.

Using the plans and checklists as prompts, look at each area or section of the business including outside the buildings, and note the following:

◆ Which individuals regularly work in that area.

◆ Relief staff or people who cover for breaks.

◆ Who has to use the area for access or as a route between sections.

◆ Customers or clients that may be there at any particular time, even if only for short periods.

◆ Where sub-contractors or temporary staff are used, especially if they are likely to bring additional fire hazard materials with them.

◆ Work experience or young people working on site.

◆ Passers-by who might be at risk if a fire started.

Also note the location of individuals who could experience difficulties with escape if a fire starts, such as:

◆ Elderly or frail people.

◆ Wheelchair users or those with restricted mobility.

◆ Pregnant women, parents with small children, or unaccompanied children.

Note areas that are rarely used, largely unoccupied, or where a fire could go unnoticed before the alarm was raised. You must also consider where the most vulnerable areas are for arson attacks, especially near perimeter fences or where flammable materials and scrap are stored.

Severity of harm

In relation to fire, the severity of harm that could occur is principally the same in most situations, and cannot readily be related to whether the person is carrying out one activity rather than another.

If a fire starts and people cannot escape in time, the result could be burns, asphyxiation or being overcome by smoke and toxic fumes, or major injury while trying to escape from above ground level.

The severity of harm can be related to other things – will several people or just one or two individuals be harmed; is there danger of explosion? Another measure might be the impact of a fire on other businesses in the vicinity.

What's next door?

It is vital that you know if adjoining businesses use highly flammable or volatile substances or processes, that they have assessed the risks and have sufficient controls of their own in place.

The following is a useful way to consider the potential severity of a fire if one started:

1 A small-scale fire that could be tackled safely in the early stages by a competent person; very localised.

2 A localised fire to start with, but could spread very quickly.

3 A localised fire to start with, but one that could quickly produce toxic smoke and fumes.

4 A fire that would quickly spread over a wide area, perhaps via a spread of chemicals or other highly combustible materials or dusts.

5 Significant risk of explosion.

Likelihood of fire

Closely linked with the potential severity of harm is the likelihood that it will occur, and what steps you have taken to reduce this likelihood. The main considerations are:

◆ Whether a fire is likely to start.

◆ What controls are in place to reduce the chances of it starting.

◆ How will people know it has started.

◆ How can they escape.

Apply the same sort of risk ratings in the same way you did for health and safety. The question of whether it is unlikely/likely/very likely that a fire will occur is similar to the criteria used in previous risk assessments, although the criteria for the severity of harm is based on the list above.

Priorities for taking further action

The risk table has changed, with more columns to show the potential severity of the fire, and additional criteria of number of people likely to be affected.

Risk table 2. Assessing the fire risks

	Slow burning localised	Rapid spread localised	Toxic smoke localised	Rapid spread widely	Explosion
Few people affected	1	1	2	2	3
Highly unlikely	1	1	2	3	4
Likely	2	2	3	4	4
Very likely	2	3	4	4	5
Many people affected	3	4	4	5	5

This is just one way you might give some rating values. It is a subjective way to consider the risks, but does provide a starting point to consider priorities. Ratings represent:

  5 = Extremely high risk

3–4 = Medium risk

1–2 = Low risk.

Existing fire controls

Following the same procedure as before, note the existing controls in place to reduce the risks to people if a fire starts, and then to identify further actions needed where controls are insufficient.

These will vary according to size of business premises are, industry sector and other variables, so could be a fairly short list. Here are the main things likely to be in place already.

Detection systems

Smoke or heat alarms are triggered by a rise in smoke or heat in a location. They should be positioned to detect a change in the atmosphere as soon as possible and allow a potential source of fire to be identified quickly so that premises can be vacated if necessary.

Alarms

Once a potential fire is detected, other alarms can be triggered to alert people. These can range from a handbell in very small workplace, to electrically operated alarm systems that warn people on site and alert the fire service at the same time.

Can people in the workplace be warned quickly enough to escape safely if a fire starts? Given the risks you have identified, is an automatic alarm system needed, or is a manually operated alarm sufficient?

Signs and notices

You should have notices displayed to tell people what to do if a fire starts and they hear the alarm, even if these are very simple notices.

Remember that if there is a lot of smoke, people easily become disoriented and frightened to move through it to safety, so it is vital that people know where to go and have practised the drill for escaping quickly.

Exit routes or means of escape

Note where fire doors and fire exits are located. In particular, make sure doors are not locked, are easily and quickly opened in an emergency, and that they do actually lead people to safety!

Exit routes and doors must be kept clear of rubbish, goods or other obstructions at all times, so check that this is actually the case. They must be well lit, on an independent power supply (may just be battery operated), and preferably with some form of lighting near floor level to guide people through smoke. If your assessment identifies people with mobility difficulties, there should be means of escape identified to accommodate wheelchair users too.

Fire fighting equipment

Identify where portable fire fighting equipment is located, such as fire extinguishers or fire blankets, and note distances between them – are they clearly visible, right for the type of fire that is likely, regularly maintained?

Note that people should be trained to use portable equipment correctly.

Note any other means in place for fighting a fire, such as sprinkler systems or automatic shut-down procedures.

Exit signs

The signs should tell people where fire exits are, and the quickest route to get to them. They should be clear and visible and in a language that is appropriate to the people working on or visiting site.

Further controls

While the measures above are a valuable part of the way you control the risks from fire, there may be other measures you can take that give better protection to the people you are responsible for. Some of them may already be in place, but some may need to be introduced or developed further. The three main elements of control are:

1   RD – reducing the likelihood that a fire will occur.

2   EP – preparing for an emergency.

3   AA – taking appropriate action if a fire has started.

Reducing the likelihood of fire

How likely is it that a fire will start in a given area where the three parts of the fire triangle (ignition source, fuel, oxygen) are present together?

Ways to reduce this likelihood include:

◆   Controlling sources of ignition.

◆   Heat-producing machines or equipment must be maintained properly, and ducts or flues kept clean.

◆   Electrical equipment should be checked regularly, circuit breakers used where appropriate, and socket points not overloaded.

◆   Replace heaters that have a naked flame with convector heaters or central heating systems (and check with your insurers if you use portable gas heaters).

◆   Smoking policy and procedures for hot work, such as welding or flame cutting, should be enforced properly, especially the use of matches or lighters.

◆   Thorough checking procedures at the end of the working day, or in areas of low occupation.

◆   Reducing potential fuel sources.

◆   Replace flammable substances or materials with less hazardous ones.

◆   Change the way substances and materials are used in processes.

- Keep the smallest workable volume at the point of production, rather than very large amounts, and transfer materials in a safe manner.

- Use fire-resisting cabinets to store highly flammable liquids and substances, and keep them separate from other flammable substances.

- Good housekeeping and proper disposal of waste products can significantly reduce potential risk, especially opportunities for arson attacks.

- Reducing potential sources of oxygen.

- Simple actions, like keeping doors and windows closed where appropriate.

- Check that oxygen or similar cylinders are stored safely and with proper ventilation.

- Make sure substances that act as oxidising agents are stored away from heat sources and flammable substances.

- Make sure that materials or substances that could help to spread the fire are not stored too closely together.

- The building structure itself may help the spread of fire, with hidden roof cavities or large, open plan areas, as may furnishings or furniture, so include these in your assessments.

Preparing for an emergency

You can take precautions like those listed above to try and reduce the chances that a fire will start. Unfortunately fires do occur so you also need to make sure that you and your workers know what to do if one does.

The procedures you have in place should include:

- Establish a realistic and effective plan of action that will safeguard people, incorporating warning people, escaping from the premises and fighting a fire.

- Make sure everyone on site knows what to do if there is a fire, especially where you have new or temporary workers on site.

- Regularly test the plan to check that it works, and that people do remember what they have been told to do.

- Make sure your emergency procedures are known by others who may share the work premises, and do not conflict with procedures they have. Make sure you are also informed about their plans, particularly any significant fire hazards they have that could pose a serious risk to your business.

- Ensure the emergency plan includes reference to checking and maintaining equipment, alarms, and exit routes or doors. This includes checking at close of shift, and security measures to reduce opportunities for arson attacks or trespass.

- People must be trained adequately, training up-dated as required, whether in safe systems of work, using fire fighting equipment, or first aid training. It should also include shutting down machinery in an emergency, fire marshals and contacting the emergency services.

Action if a fire has started

This is primarily about warning people that there is a fire, ensuring they can escape safely, and preventing the spread of fire where possible.

- Make sure the alarm can be raised, and that people can see it and hear it, particularly if it is a noisy workplace or individuals have sight or hearing difficulties. If there are few people on-site, with just one main working area, it could well be sufficient to raise the alarm by shouting 'Fire!' or by using a hand bell.

- Ensure escape routes and exit doors are adequate, clearly signposted, and well lit. The exits must, of course, lead people to safety so check that this is the case whatever the time of day you are working. For example, if your fire exit leads to an outside courtyard that is open to the public during the day but has perimeter gates that are locked for security purposes after dark, people could be trapped in the event of a fire.

- Make sure someone has responsibility for alerting the fire brigade, checking the buildings have been fully evacuated and people are at a safe muster point, and for providing the fire fighters with information about the hazards on site. A 'grab bag' with this information (plus torch, whistle, reflective jacket, walkie-talkie or phone) is a useful method.

- Simple actions that prevent the spread of fire include keeping the door closed where a fire has been sighted, turning off electricity supplies if necessary (but not if it then puts people in further danger), and keeping fire doors closed.

Although this section has been a little different, the principles are the same in that hazards have been identified, risks to people been assessed, and control measures considered to reduce the risks as much as possible.

The same process can be used to assess risks in relation to other aspects of the business, such as environmental or food safety risks.

6 Managing risks

Preparing to manage

Up until now, this has been an auditing process to identify just where you are at the moment in relation to health, safety and fire risks. You have plans of the site and premises, and a range of checklists to identify how well you are controlling risks in the workplace by:

◆ Identifying health, safety and fire hazards in each area of the business.

◆ Identifying the people likely to be injured or harmed by these hazards, plus any individuals or groups of people that may be particularly vulnerable.

◆ Assessing the potential risks to workers and others who could be on site at any particular time.

◆ Reviewing existing controls that are in place to reduce the risks, and identifying further control measures that may be necessary.

While this is an excellent beginning, and demonstrates to others that you are taking these risks to health and safety seriously, we have not yet:

◆ Decided any future targets or objectives for you and the business.

◆ Considered their order of priority.

◆ Produced a plan to take them forward.

◆ Identified ways to check whether you have met the targets or to measure the success of your efforts.

These elements of managing the risks successfully are just as important as those of identifying the risks people face. You are required by law to actually *manage* health, safety and fire risks to workers and others in your business, so must take the work done so far still further forward.

Priorities

Using your checklists and risk tables, identify where actions are needed to reduce risks further, which processes or activity areas are involved, which people are affected, and any areas of overlap between the three risk factors that need to be addressed.

1 First pick out all the factors you decided were **kigh risk/likelihood** against safety, health and fire hazards.

   ◆ Against each one in turn, check whether **controls were assessed as adequate**. If they were, just make a note **'Review'** when conditions change significantly, or in one year at most.

   ◆ If the **controls were seen as inadequate** for safety, health or fire hazards, and therefore you need to take action, check whether more than one area of risk needs attention so that you can deal with it at the same time.

   ◆ Give **Priority rating 1** (we are not deciding actual order that actions will be taken yet, just rating them by importance) for all those from high risk/ likelihood that need action.

2 Follow the same procedure to pick out **medium risk/likelihood** factors. If controls are adequate, mark them for review, and if not check against all three safety, health, fire risk categories. Put **Priority rating 2** against each of these.

3 Follow the same procedure to pick out **low risk/likelihood** factors identified, marking for review or checking against other risk categories as necessary. Put **Priority rating 3** against these.

Don't ignore the low risks

Any factors considered low risk or trivial may not necessarily be assessed as perfectly controlled, so will still need to be reviewed in the future and might still need some action such as refresher training for operators, or new signs, etc.

Plan of action

You now have a priority listing of:

1   Urgent attention required, do as soon as possible.

2   Keep a close watch on the situation, take action as quickly as possible.

3   Keep a close watch on the situation, plan what action is to take place.

You can now set targets and produce a plan of action to show what you intend to do. Use Checklist 7 as a guide alongside your list of all the actions needed. Start with all the Priority 1 factors.

There may, of course, be just two or three things that need to be done, or quite a long list of fairly urgent measures that are needed. You cannot do everything at the same time, and some may require significant investment of time or resources to put right. You might also need to get specialist professional advice on things like noise or air contamination levels before you can decide what the most appropriate actions will be.

It is quite likely that there will be a list of steps that need to be taken before you can meet a particular target. For instance, if new storage facilities are needed, because of either a fire or safety hazard, you may need to get professional advice about exactly what you need, look at a range of suitable products, decide which one will be right for you, and place an order.

You will also need to prepare the area where new storage will be installed, install the new facility and finally reassess the situation to confirm that controls are now adequate.

Follow up is essential

You have a duty to assess the risks and have adequate controls in place, so you do have to do something to follow up your assessments. As with any business targets, proper planning with timescales and clear measures to judge success is essential. Identify timescales for reviewing health, safety and fire risk assessments to make sure control measures are still appropriate and effective.

Checklist 7: Managing the Risks

Management Actions taken:	Yes (tick)	Complete by	Review date	Review by
Established priorities: · noted "Review" where controls adequate · identified high risk factors with Priority Rating 1 · identified medium risk factors with Priority Rating 2 · identified low risk factors with Priority Rating 3				
a) Prepared Plan of Action, with steps needed and timescales set for completion, for · Priority Rating 1 · Priority Rating 2 · Priority Rating 3				
b) Established appropriate records				
c) Provided staff with relevant and sufficient information				
d) Established appropriate consultation procedures with workers				
e) Identified one or more competent person(s) for H&S				
f) Arranged methods for keeping up to date with legislation changes				
g) Prepared a Health and Safety Policy				
h) Included other policy statements where appropriate				

Further actions that form part of this section are:

◆ Assess potential hazards and risks if you change the product, process or equipment.

◆ Make sure that new equipment or machinery is safe when you buy it, suitable for its intended use and does not introduce other hazards.

◆ Set targets for health and safety.

◆ Make sure that working safely is accepted as relevant and the norm in the business, with you/the owner of the firm setting an example and sticking to it!

Records you should keep

These include:

- Maintenance checks on machinery or equipment. In some cases, you are legally required to keep records of such checks, for example, on lifting gear and hoists; plus those on on portable electrical equipment and on fire-fighting equipment.

- Results of noise level and hearing tests, air-borne contaminants, etc.

- Hazard data sheets that tell you about using and storing hazardous substances.

- Accident and first aid records, especially details of serious injury, diseases, or dangerous occurrences that have to be reported under RIDDOR (Reporting of Injuries, Diseases, Dangerous Occurrences Regulations, i.e. notifying HSE of these by phone/form/on-line.)

- Sickness absence records.

- Details of accident investigations carried out internally. Include near-miss incidents too if you can, as they often suggest where there is an accident waiting to happen which then becomes foreseeable.

Why investigate accidents?

The aim of accident investigation is to get to the root cause of the incident, to make sure it does not happen again. It can also identify potentially vulnerable individuals, areas where further controls need to be introduced, and situations where existing controls need to be reinforced. It is, therefore, an important element of showing that you are managing health and safety effectively.

- Records of individual workers' skills and expertise, plus training received and planned for the future.

- Names of qualified first aid staff and where they are generally located, details of those trained to use fire-fighting equipment, and individuals responsible for acting as fire wardens or notifying emergency services.

- Health monitoring and surveillance records for individual workers, where necessary. (These are confidential and must be kept secure.)

Informing and involving staff

This is a crucial part of both national and EU legislation, so should not be ignored or left to chance. All workers, including temporary, part-time, contract staff, must be informed about potential hazards, the risks of injury or harm associated with them, and controls that are in place to safeguard individuals. Involve people working in the different areas on site when identifying hazards, as they will be more familiar with them on a day-to-day basis than someone from outside.

If new hazards or risks to health are identified, you must tell people and make sure they know and understand the safeguards that are in place to protect them. It is not enough to just tell them to read a notice or leaflet.

Relevant warning or information notices must be displayed where necessary, clearly and in a language or format that is easily understood by the people they are aimed at.

You are obliged to display the HSE 'Health and Safety Law Poster' and details of public and employer liability insurance cover you hold.

Approaches to consultation

By law, you must consult with staff on issues of health and safety. This does NOT mean you have to have a formal Health and Safety Committee structure in place in a very small, close-knit firm where it is obviously inappropriate. However, you DO have to have some method for talking to workers, discussing health and safety issues or concerns, and agreeing future actions to ensure the safety of all. This could be by talking directly with all workers together as a group, or in a larger company by discussing issues or concerns through an elected workers' representative. You must remember to include off-site workers or those working outside normal business hours too.

Competent people

A 'competent person' in the context of health and safety, should:

- Know and understand what they need to do.

- Have the technical skills to be able to do it.

- Have sufficient expertise in the subject area to be able to carry out the tasks to the required level.

- Have sufficient resources and the authority as well as the responsibility to do it.

Many aspects of risk assessment do not need to be carried out by highly qualified OH&S professionals. You can do a large amount of the work yourself, and it may be preferable to use existing internal staff where possible. On the other hand, there are some jobs that you cannot do without the relevant expertise, such as eye tests, noise and hearing assessments, assessing levels of contamination, identifying potentially hazardous properties of substances, or individual health surveillance.

People need to be trained in first aid and fire-fighting techniques, and in some cases hold specific qualifications for using certain equipment or machinery. There are a variety of qualifications available in health and safety, but many are aimed at professionals rather than people taking on the responsibilities as part of other roles. In any event, people need some guidance and training if they are to take on such responsibilities.

Individual responsibilities for health and safety

The owner/managing director of the firm has ultimate responsibility for ensuring the safety, health and welfare of workers, and cannot escape this by making someone else the nominated person with responsibility for health and safety.

Every individual in the firm has some responsibility, whether as an employee, self-employed contractor, or as part of the management team. Everyone must know this and be given appropriate training and support to be able to carry out their responsibilities. This includes Induction training when they join the firm or come onto your site (even as temporary workers), plus adequate training in the correct procedures for carrying out their job in a safe and healthy manner.

Keeping up to date

This is a concern for all businesses as the employer must take responsibility for the damage, injury or ill-health that results from work activities. It is complicated still further by the increasing overlap of legislation between health, safety, environment, fire, employment protection and public health.

There is a wide range of resources available to help firms keep up-to-date with changes in legislation. These include:

Government reference sources:

- The Health and Safety Executive (HSE) has an excellent website where you can access details of regulations, guidance and publications (free or priced) www.hse.gov.uk and www.hsebooks.co.uk

- The Health & Safety Authority (HAS) in Ireland

- The Home Office for further guidance on fire.

- Stationery Office (previously HMSO) www.tsoshop.co.uk

- UK government site to access other departments: www.open.gov.uk

- Your local authority for the environmental health office.

Organisations and professional bodies:

- Loss Prevention Council

- Fire Protection Association

- Arson Prevention Bureau

- Chartered Institute of Environmental Health (CIEH)

- Institution of Occupational Health (IOSH)

- Royal Society for the Prevention of Accidents (RoSPA)

- British Standards Institute

- Trades Union Congress (TUC)

- Trade associations (there may be one for your industry sector),

- British Chambers of Commerce (BCC) and your local chamber of commerce

- Confederation of British Industry (CBI)
- Federation of Small Businesses (FSB)
- Magazines and journals
- Tolley *Health & Safety at Work* journal (Butterworth's)
- BizHot Business Hotline Publications *Directors' Briefings*
- Journals and magazines issued by professional bodies and institutes (they can be accessed via their websites or generally at local college or university libraries).

Know your legislation!

You have a duty to make sure you comply with health, safety and fire legislation relevant to your business, so you must ensure that you know what that legislation actually is. This could be a huge task, and could easily keep someone in your firm in full-time employment for the whole year! Clearly this is not a realistic option for most firms, so you will have to identify the sources of information that are most accessible and relevant to you.

It is not necessarily the detail of the legislation you need to know, but rather the underlying principles and purposes, and the actions you need to take to ensure compliance.

8 Your H&S policy

Drawing up a policy statement

By law, you must have a policy on health and safety whatever size your firm, but only need a written version if you employ five or more people. However, as we have seen, there are likely to be other groups of people who want to see evidence that you have a policy, such as your insurance provider, or clients/suppliers when you tender or contract with them.

Start with a general statement of your policy related to health and safety, such as your commitment to safeguarding the health and safety of workers. You should include with this the names of people in the firm who have specific responsibilities, details of how and where they can be contacted, and contact details for external sources of advice, support or services. It should include those responsible for carrying out risk assessments, maintaining machinery, providing training to staff, supervising evacuation of the building, providing First Aid treatment, etc.

Other policy statements to include

You could also include references to, or outlines of, your policy on:

♦ Smoking, and restricted areas where it is permitted or banned.

♦ Use of drugs or alcohol on premises.

♦ Disability and rehabilitation of workers.

♦ Lone workers.

♦ Stress, bullying or harassment in the workplace.

♦ Staff training plans.

♦ Emergency plans.

Consider how you will deal with people who are absent for long periods, due to illness or injury caused by work, and how you can help them back into work as they recover, i.e. a rehabilitation policy. In small firms this is not easy, but there is pressure from government and the insurance industry to make employers take on more of the costs of long-term illness. You also have responsibility for outworkers or homeworkers employed by you, so they should be included in your process for identifying risks, and appropriate control measures discussed with them.

Approaches to managing H&S

There are different approaches to managing health and safety risks, including formal systems such as:

- HSG65 published by the HSE – this is the approach taken here, and it forms the basis of assessing health, safety and fire risks.

- BSI British Standard 8800 – aimed at small businesses, it incorporates both the HSG65 and the ISO 14000 (see below) approaches.

- ISO 14000 Environmental Management Standard takes a Plan – Do – Check – Think approach, which emphasises the continuous improvement focus of monitor and review – fits with ISO 9000 series for managing quality.

Whichever system you already have, or choose to introduce, the main principles of effective H&S management are:

- Making sure that all people in the organisation know their own and others' responsibilities for working safely and healthily.

- A policy statement for H&S management that covers all areas of risk, including workers on and off site.

- Clear senior management commitment to action.

- Maintaining adequate and appropriate records of hazards, controls and systems in place to protect people.

- Involving and informing staff throughout the risk assessment process, and making sure they know of any substantial risks to their safety or health.

- Appropriate training and supervision for staff.

- Use of outside H&S specialists where necessary to work with anyone internally deemed as a 'competent person'.

- Other policy statements that link with H&S policy.

Review

In the same way that producing a business plan is not a one-off activity, the management of health and safety and other risks is an ongoing process. Your policy will, therefore, change over time as the business itself changes, and certainly the results of risk assessments will need to be reviewed and updated regularly.

Review the activities carried out so far. Although all aspects of business activity are covered here, it is likely that you only need to consider maybe one or two departments. The approach is the same although clearly there will be greater involvement of others if you are working in a larger organisation.

The critical element of successful management of health, safety and fire risks is to monitor what is happening regularly, and always review risk assessments when processes or procedures change, staff move from one section to another, or when the law changes. If you are studying for an examination in OH&S, the principles covered in the Learning Made Simple guide should provide a sound base for your studies.

The way to ensure that the management of risks is carried out effectively in your business is to make sure that the commitment at the very top of the firm is real, and that health and safety is treated as an integral part of how you run the business.

It is not just about what the law requires, but should be treated in the same way as other management issues, such as financial management and marketing. It should be very clear by now just how much it actually does influence those other issues.

Industry sector examples

Office-based businesses

These are generally considered to be 'low risk' environments.

Safety

- Storage facilities - overcrowding; inadequate for weight; inaccessible corners, cupboards; goods piled too high so danger of items falling; too high up, especially for heavy boxes or files, so people tempted to stand on chairs, etc. to reach.

- Minor cuts from paper edges, use of scissors, using wrong tools to open boxes or parcels; injury from use of guillotines, shredders.

- Slips and trips - trailing cables; drawers left open in desks and cabinets; boxes stored under and around desks; poor floor surfaces, worn carpet especially at edges; stairs obstructed or poorly lit.

- Wet floors in lobby areas, kitchens.

- Electric shock or burns - overloaded sockets; incorrect fuses; damaged cables; electrical equipment not serviced adequately; kettles on draining boards.

- Manual handling injuries, from lifting, pulling, pushing heavy or awkwardly shaped items.

- Violence to staff in firms dealing with sensitive or confidential information.

Health

- Use of Visual Display Units (VDUs) - see notes pages 43-44.

- Lighting - adequate for the type of work, to reduce eye strain and poor posture, and reduce reflections or flicker.

- Hazardous substances such as inks and solvents; cleaning materials.

- Stress - especially if threat of violence, heavy workloads, tight deadlines, insufficient staff, inadequate rest breaks and facilities.

Fire

- Electrical faults; overloaded sockets; poor maintenance of portable electrical equipment.

- Fuel sources such as paper (especially when shredded and less densely packed), solvents, etc.

This appendix highlights some specific hazards and risks associated with certain industry sectors. Many of these are common to several industries, but are still worth noting separately. It is not an exhaustive list, and you should seek further guidance if there are specific things you are worried about in your own company.

Small retail premises

Safety

- Goods stored incorrectly after delivery until they can be put away; shelving and racking systems inadequate and not strong enough; goods are stored at inappropriate height; trucks or trolleys not available to move goods. See page 29..

- Opening boxes and containers – cuts and injuries likely from use or misuse of incorrect tools; plastic band ties and injuries to hands.

- Slips and trips – discarded packaging; trailing cables and leads; poor, uneven floor surfaces; wet floors in main shop and storage areas; aisles and passages blocked/obstructed; unsafe steps and stairs.

- Falling items – from shelves; collapse of racks or shelves; goods stacked too high or incorrectly.

- Injuries from use of machines, such as display goods, compacters, shredders.

- Electric shock from portable electrical equipment; damaged cables.

- Theft and violence to staff – especially vulnerable lone workers, or those locking up/opening premises; paying money in at the bank.

Health

- Stress from threat of violence; long working hours; dealing with the public.

- Back injuries from incorrect manual handling techniques.

- Tiredness from standing all shift, without proper breaks or opportunity to sit down.

- Contamination of foods and health risks.

- Use of chemical substances for cleaning; storage of substances on sales shelves; damaged packaging on delivery or in storage.

Fire

- Smoking by staff or customers – discarded cigarettes or matches.

- Electrical faults, overloaded sockets, damaged cables.

- Stacked cardboard or other rubbish a source of fuel.

- Products may be highly flammable, or act as fuel if fire starts.

- Arson, especially where rubbish or other goods stacked.

- Spread of fire likely to be rapid in crowded areas.

Take note

Escape routes must be kept clear at all times. You must have proper emergency procedures, and staff adequately trained to carry them out.

Hairdressers, beauticians and similar

Safety

- Use of portable electrical equipment – danger of electric shock, especially in wet conditions.
- Burns to staff and customers from hairdryers, infra-red lamps and other equipment.
- Scalds from hot water.
- Slips and trips – wet, slippery floors; trailing wires from hand-held equipment; hair and waste materials on floor; customers' bags, etc. on floor; unsafe steps or poor floor surfaces in premises; poor lighting.
- Children and hazards such as them pulling equipment down by cables; touching hot items such as curling tongs; causing trip hazard with toys, etc.
- Burns from use of chemicals in preparations.

Health

- Storage of chemicals.
- Use of substances – fumes can affect eyes, lungs, skin; inhalation from bleach- based products; sensitisers.
- Dermatitis and other skin reactions from direct contact with substances; burns from direct contact or splashes on skin or in eyes; hazard still present when discarding waste papers, cotton wool, etc.
- Back and leg strain from standing for long periods, or twisting actions.
- RSI from repetitive actions such as cutting hair.

Fire

- Explosion from aerosol cans.
- Infra-red lamps a source of heat/ ignition.
- Chemical substances in combination can cause fire hazard; ferocity of fire increased by presence of substances.
- Alcohol in some dye preparations make them highly flammable.
- Oxidising agents in some preparations provide the additional oxygen.

Tip

Aerosol cans pose special risks. Store them away from direct sunlight, and preferably in a fire-resistant cabinet. If a fire starts, inform firemen where they are in the premises.

Textiles, dressmaking, furnishings

Safety

- Injury from use of cutting tools, hand-held manual or powered tools.

- Use of sewing machines, and danger of fingers or clothes being trapped; injury from moving parts and needles, especially on larger industrial machines.

- Burns from ironing, pressing; scalds from steaming or other processes.

- Slips and trips – crowded conditions; work in progress at each work station; cables; materials stored incorrectly (insufficient storage facilities).

- Storage of heavy materials; danger of falling objects.

- Sharp objects, pins, etc.

Health

- RSI – especially using scissors and sewing actions, particularly due to speed of working; hands, arms, upper body affected, made worse by twisting in seat.

- Eye strain, due to long periods of work activity – need for adequate lighting, breaks, proper equipment for job.

- Back injuries due to incorrect manual handling, especially pulling, pushing, lifting heavy awkward loads; need for correct seating; specific needs of pregnant women.

- Fumes from some processes such as mercerising, and residual fumes from dyeing processes; causing skin/eye/throat/lung irritation or acting as sensitiser.

- Noise levels – especially as likely to be over prolonged periods, and background as well as local source.

- Stress – due to speed of work; piecework; team work and pressure to work to level of the quickest person; inadequate training; volume of work.

- Inadequate ventilation – build up of heat and dust causing discomfort and breathing problems.

Fire

- Fibres and dust in the air, danger of explosion and rapid spread if fire starts.

- Electrical equipment and sparks; proper maintenance needed.

- Heating appliances, especially portable or old and inefficient models; overcrowding of premises.

- Flammable fabrics and materials to provide fuel for a fire; particular danger of toxic fumes or smoke produced.

- Storage and usage of chemicals for different processes; cleaning materials and lubricants for machines.

- Emergency procedures not in place; exits obstructed.

Take note

Fire warning systems are particularly important in those little used places where fire could smoulder unnoticed for some time.

Mobile services

These include chiropodist, hairdresser, dog grooming and similar services.

Safety

- Personal safety on other people's premises, including danger presented by people or animals.
- Injury from carrying equipment or materials.
- Injury to client from processes or materials used.
- Portable electrical equipment – faulty supplies or sockets; faulty or damaged equipment.
- Slips and trips – working in unsuitable and unfamiliar surroundings.

Health

- Manual handling injuries to back, carrying equipment and materials.
- Other musculoskeletal injuries due to posture during work; possible RSI.
- Hygiene and contamination through skin/ingestion/inhalation; insufficient washing facilities available.

Fire

- Storage of chemicals and other substances at home.
- Electrical faults.
- Explosion from use of aerosol cans.

Take note

Insurance cover must be adequate for equipment and materials at home or on others' premises.

Florist

Safety

- Use of wire cutting tools; heavy duty cutting tools for plant materials.
- Scratches, cuts, and puncture injuries from plant materials.
- Slips and trips – water spillages; obstructions such as flower bins in aisles or work areas; trailing wires; poor floor surfaces, overcrowded areas.
- Shock from electrical equipment in wet conditions; hazards from localised heating appliances.
- Buying and delivery of bulky supplies – handling injuries; storage facilities.
- Driving hazards when making deliveries to customers.

Health

- Tetanus, allergic reactions and other diseases from handling plants.
- Handling and storage of hazardous chemicals for care of plants; potential for allergy sensitisers.
- RSI, with small repetitive movements; posture and standing for long periods.
- Temperature and humidity, especially working in cool conditions.
- Stress – contract work, emergency work for funerals, for example; weddings; dealing with and advising customers.

Fire

- Combustible materials such as dried foliage, packaging materials.

Tip

Often seen as a low-risk business, florists do in fact face significant hazards during a normal working day, frequently using temporary or part-time staff to help. Conditions can be even worse if the business operates from a market stall where all stock and materials have to be transported to and from the pitch each day. It is important to establish safe working practices right from the start.

Repairers of small items

These include repairers of jewellery, watches, dentures or shoes and the like.

Safety

- Use of fine drilling or abrasive equipment.
- Flying pieces of metal or other materials in eyes.
- Danger of burns from materials or process.
- Use of small, hand-held cutting tools; keep them sharp and well maintained.
- Portable electrical equipment and electric shock.
- Small-scale soldering or welding.

Health

- Eye sight at risk with close work; need for adequate lighting in work areas; may need 'daylight' bulbs or measures to reduce glare.
- Posture at work bench, especially when carrying out close work over long periods of time.
- Use of hazardous substances, including solvents, adhesives, and cleaning materials; irritant or damage to skin, eyes, throat or lungs.

- Fumes produced by soldering or welding; need for adequate PPE.
- Appropriate ventilation systems needed.

Fire

- Chemical substances and rapid spread of fire.
- Fumes from processes; build up of fumes from open containers.
- Storage of hazardous substances.
- Flammable fine dusts and powders and danger of explosion.
- Electrical faults, heat sources, sparks as ignition source.
- Flammable materials as fuel if fire starts.

Take note

For shoe repairers, there will be additional safety factors associated with large pieces of machinery, such as punches, stapling machines, and edge trimmers. All are extremely hazardous so will need to be considered in the same way as those in engineering.

Tip

Repairers, like retailers, need to be alert to risks to customers on the premises.

Pottery

Making

Safety

- Electric shocks from portable electrical equipment; insulation in wet conditions.
- Cuts, crush injuries from moving parts of machinery for example, cutters, kneaders, mixers.
- Unsafe racking and storage systems, especially in relation to height and weight of loads stored; danger of falling objects.
- Slips and trips - wet floors, especially with clay; trailing hoses and cables; materials stored on floor.

Health

- Lighting levels; eye strain from prolonged fine or detailed work.
- Hazardous substances in clays, paints, etc. - e.g. lead, selenium, cobalt, silicon.
- Restriction of access for pregnant or nursing women.
- Temperature and humidity levels; need for proper ventilation.
- Use of cleaning materials, irritants to skin and eyes, inhalation and lung damage.

Fire

- Electrical faults and equipment.
- Storage of materials as fuel source.
- Dusts and fumes and danger of explosion.

Kilns

Safety

- Burns from direct contact with kiln.
- Electrical shock from faulty equipment or systems; overloading sockets.
- Trapped or crushed by moving parts when loading or unloading; falling objects.

Health

- Manual handling when pulling, pushing, lifting heavy awkward loads.
- Noise levels, especially from ventilation or exhaust systems.
- Inadequate ventilation, fumes from furnaces and some processes.
- Insulation in some kilns may include asbestos or other hazardous mineral fibres.

Fire

- Use of natural gas or LPG to fire kiln as ignition/heat source.
- Storage of fuels.
- Naked flame, e.g. pilot light, as ignition source.
- Build-up of gas around the kiln, explosion or toxic fumes.
- Wooden ceilings above kilns at risk from intense heat.

Dentists

Safety

- Use of portable and permanent electrical equipment; electric shock in wet conditions.
- Use of hypodermic syringes; danger of puncture wounds to staff and patients.
- Incorrect use of drugs and anaesthetic procedures.
- Personal safety and violence from uncontrolled patients, possibly drug-induced behaviour.

Health

- Contact with transmittable diseases by breathing; skin; saliva or blood samples.
- Posture, sometimes in awkward twisting position; back strain.
- Inadequate lighting at point of work.
- Use of X-ray machines; note vulnerable workers such as pregnant women or those of child-bearing age.
- Use of VDUs and computer systems (see also Office-based businesses, page 92).

Fire

- Use and storage of chemical substances.
- Additional oxygen supplies; storage and disposal of cylinders.

Tip

Health sector workers are generally very aware of clinical safety measures for patients and staff, but not general health, safety and fire risks for the workplace as a whole. Using the site plan to identify hazards is particularly useful for this type of environment.

Vets and animal establishments

Most of the items listed for dentists also apply to vets and others working with animals. Those listed below are additional.

Safety

◆ Potential for crush/gore/bite/sting injuries from handling animals.

◆ Badly stacked materials, foodstuffs, etc. and danger of falling objects.

◆ Falls off steps, ladders; falls from animals.

Health

◆ Use and storage of chemicals or drugs, many of which are stronger for use with animals than for humans.

◆ Inadequate eye and skin protection; inhalation of some preparations particularly harmful.

◆ Manual handling injuries with bales of hay, animal foodstuffs, animal equipment such as saddles.

◆ Diseases passed from animals to humans (zoonoses), tetanus, presence of pesticides.

◆ Use of X-ray machines, radiation.

Take note

Workers need suitable protective clothing and access to adequate washing and cleaning facilities.

Fire

◆ Highly combustible foodstuffs and hay.

Tip

It is important to make sure that hazard data sheets are available from all product suppliers and that safe procedures are followed correctly every time products are stored, used or disposed of.

Agriculture and horticulture

Safety

- Accidents with vehicles on site; use of trailers, bailers, harvesters.
- Rough terrain vehicles and tractors – overturning.
- Cutting or sawing equipment and large machinery – crushing/cutting/ amputation hazards.
- Use of hand-held tools and equipment; electric shock from faulty equipment, supplies or voltage.
- Falling into large containers such as silos, tanks, pits.
- Working in confined spaces.
- Storage areas; falling objects; collapse of stored goods and shelving.
- Use of pressure equipment.
- Use of ladders; working at heights inside and outside buildings.
- Crush/gore/bite/kick injuries when handling animals.
- Particular hazards associated with children on site, and when working alone in isolated area.
- Handling guns and ammunition.

Health

- Asthma and other respiratory illnesses.
- Skin, eyes and other organs may become sensitised to particular chemicals.
- Stress can be a significant risk in agriculture sectors.

Fire

- LPG and oil fuel storage and use.
- Explosion hazard from dusts and grains.
- Storage of hazardous substances, chemicals, fertilisers; storage of diesel and petrol for vehicles.
- Highly combustible materials like hay stacked in large quantities, so rapid spread of fire.
- Potential fire sources often close to living accommodation.
- Ammunition.
- Rubbish and other waste materials; arson.

Take note

Any significant risk areas need proper lighting, fencing and/or guarding to prevent unauthorised/unsupervised access, especially by children.

Forestry

Safety

- Use of chain saws - maintenance; training; guards; sharpening; brakes; correct PPE including helmet/ear defenders/goggles/gloves/leg protection/boots/no loose clothing. NOT to be used when working alone.

- Use of circular and other saws - using push sticks; proper guards in place; grippers; blades sharpened; speed set correctly; working height set properly.

- Shredding machines - correct guards in place and correct use of push sticks.

- Ladders, lifting gear in good working order and regularly checked; use of harnesses.

- Hazards of overhead electricity cables; electric shock from faulty or damaged electrical equipment; incorrect voltages.

- Use of barriers and warning signs to protect others.

- Escape routes identified beforehand; pre-plan risk zones, ground conditions, wind direction, etc.

- Use of hand tools for digging, planting.

- Loading wood onto vehicles - securing the weight correctly, ground conditions suitable for vehicle when loading; dangers associated with transporting load.

Health

- Manual handling of heavy, awkward loads, and danger of back injuries.

- Noise from use of machines.

- Dusts - especially highly carcinogenic hard wood dusts.

- Use of or contact with wood treatments, preservatives, other hazardous chemicals.

- Use of or contact with pesticides, fungicides, herbicides.

Fire

- Sparks from use of electrical equipment.

- Highly combustible materials, with potential for rapid spread with small shavings, etc. and intensity of fire from stacked materials.

- Risk of fire or explosion from use and storage of chemical substances.

- Risk of fire or explosion from use and storage of oil and petrol products used in vehicles.

Tip

In forestry, most hazards arise from not doing things properly. Safety starts with the proper maintenance and use of machines, tools and equipment.

Carpenters and joiners

Safety

◆ Slips and trips – need for good housekeeping standards; hazards from off-cuts of materials; trailing cable, leads, ventilation or compressor hoses; wet floors from water, adhesives, solvents, etc.

◆ Use of powered tools; machines with moving parts – correct guards in place and use of push sticks.

◆ Cuts from saws, circular or band saws, other cutting tools, especially kickbacks.

◆ Electric shock from faulty or damaged electrical equipment; overloaded sockets; incorrect voltage for location; use of circuit breakers vital.

◆ Hazard from materials falling when incorrectly stored or stacked; collapse of wood stores or racking systems.

◆ Use of ladders, scaffolding, steps – regular checks, wear harnesses as appropriate, check conditions if working on someone else's site (see Window Cleaners, page 106).

Health

◆ Noise from use of some electrical or powered tools.

◆ Lighting adequate at point of work, especially if portable lighting needed.

◆ Manual handling injuries to back and upper body from working in awkward positions for long periods; carrying, lifting, pulling and pushing large, heavy or awkward loads.

◆ Dust hazards from cutting, sawing, drilling – lung/skin/throat/eye damage especially cancer from some wood dusts.

◆ Need for local exhaust systems at point of work.

◆ Use and storage of hazardous substances such as glues, wood treatments, smokes, solvents, paints; especially note potential build-up of fumes from open containers.

◆ Working in confined spaces such as floor or loft cavities – ventilation and emergency escape systems.

◆ Protection of skin from harmful rays in direct sunshine; potential for skin burns.

Fire

◆ Electric sparks from use of electrical equipment; faulty equipment or overloading sockets.

◆ Explosion from concentration of wood dusts, shavings, etc.

◆ Use and storage of flammable substances (glues, treatments, paints, solvents).

◆ Use of compressed air equipment; gas or oxygen cylinders as additional oxygen sources.

◆ Transporting hazardous substances – amounts and type of containers used.

◆ Combustible furnishing fabrics and materials, especially foam-based fillings; storage of finished goods; packaging materials.

◆ Waste rags or materials containing traces of flammable substances.

Construction

The major hazards apply to most trades on construction sites, generally in the following categories:

♦ Working at heights.

♦ Falls from or through roofs, windows, floors, stair shafts, unguarded areas.

♦ Electric shock, and use of portable electrical equipment; overhead cables or trailing leads.

♦ Injuries from moving parts when using equipment, machinery and tools.

♦ Burns from use of blow torches or other heat sources.

♦ Pressurised containers and equipment and risks of explosion.

♦ Working in confined spaces or underground workings.

♦ Manual handling - lifting, carrying or moving large/heavy/awkward loads.

♦ Effects of heat, cold, humidity, wet (including skin cancer from exposure to the sun).

♦ Use of hazardous substances - storage, handling, disposal.

♦ Vehicle safety on site, including potential for overturning.

Take note

You need to comply with the Construction Design and Management Regulations (CDM) even if you only employ two or three workers. These apply at every level of the construction project, from client, designer, planning supervisor, principal contractor and contractors right across to self-employed individuals.

Window cleaners

Safety

- Use of ladders – regular checking for signs of damage; maintenance; proper height for job; securely footed, and fixed if above first floor level; danger of side reach.

- Hazards to passers-by of falling objects; use of barriers or warning signs.

- Proper use of safety harnesses, with secure fixing to safety eyebolts.

- Falls from height, off ladders, from cradles, and from ledges or sills, etc. – adequate training in procedures and use of safety devices.

- Use of roof boards – two at a time (one to use and one to move).

- Work from scaffolding – check safety, especially if on someone else's site.

- Cuts from broken glass, through glass.

- Need to check windows, sashes, locks, etc. before starting to clean.

Health

- Use of chemicals and cleaning fluids – skin damage or breathing difficulties.

- Damage to skin from ultra violet rays when exposed directly to sun.

Take note

The HSE considers any place where a person can be injured if they fall as 'work at height' NOT just above two metres. Everything has to be based on assessment of the risk of injury or harm, so you should consider whether and how to use ladders and make sure that those working on them have received some training in the safe use of ladders. There is useful guidance on the HSE website as well as websites of relevant professional bodies and suppliers.

Butchers

Safety

- Use of knives, handsaws, cleavers – need to be well maintained, sharp, stored correctly; appropriate PPE must be worn, including chain mail apron and gloves where necessary;

- Use of cutting machines such as mincers, mixers, saws, grinders – need proper maintenance and training in use; ensure guards, locking devices, push sticks used correctly at all times.

- Slips and trips – wet floors (non-slip surfaces possible?), grease and oil products; trailing cables.

- Electric shock from faulty or damaged electrical equipment, and when used in wet conditions.

- Some machines may be 'prescribed dangerous machines' so specified steps need to be taken to protect people from the hazards.

- Need appropriate lighting to reduce potential for accidents; use of circuit breakers.

Health

- Contamination from meat and other foodstuffs (especially reference to BSE contamination).

- Manual handling injuries from heavy weights; standing for long periods; upper body damage from twisting and cutting actions.

- Use and storage of cleaning substances.

- Temperature effects, especially working in cool temperatures, or in chill rooms – slowing down of reactions and manual dexterity.

- Separation of cooked and raw meat products.

Fire

- Faulty electrical equipment; overloading sockets.

Take note

Young people are especially vulnerable in this trade. Proper training and supervision is vital.

Catering

Safety

- Injury from machinery moving parts, grinders, mixers, mincers, washing up machines, rotating-table machines (see also Butchers section).
- Use of knives, cleavers and other sharp implements.
- Burns and scalds – hot surfaces, liquids, direct heat sources in ovens and grills.
- Steam from dishwashing machines, kettles, food from microwave ovens.
- Slips and trips – wet and greasy floors; obstructions; trailing cables and hoses; storage.
- Falls – floor surfaces, steps and stairs, layout of work and customer areas, carrying heavy items, poor lighting; customers' bags, coats, etc. near tables and service area.
- Electric shock – faulty electrical equipment, insufficient maintenance, use of portable appliances; especially in wet conditions.
- Falling objects from shelves, tables; includes large equipment not anchored correctly.
- Cuts from broken glass, crockery, opened cans.
- Use of compacters, waste disposal units.
- Customer safety, especially when serving food (e.g. not over their heads).

Health

- Use of cleaning substances – skin irritants, eyes, breathing difficulties, burns.
- Food contamination during preparation; air-borne contaminants.
- Standing for long periods; silver service action of heavy weight on extended arm; pulling/pushing stacked trolleys of food or crockery.
- Adequate lighting required at workstations to reduce eyestrain; posture when carrying out close presentation or preparation work.
- Heat, cold, humidity and need for proper ventilation and exhaust systems.
- Leakage of gas fuels.
- Stress – working conditions, long hours, breaks, dealing with the public and possibly complaints.

Fire

- Electrical faults; sparks from use of electrical equipment.
- Burning fat and grease – spills, overheated, old deposits of particles.
- Other ingredients flaring during cooking under grill or on hob.
- Use and storage of LPG and other gas fuels, risk of explosion.
- Steamers or boilers and risk of explosion.
- Use and storage of aerosol cans.
- Smoking and discarded cigarettes or matches.

Hotels, guest houses and similar

Safety

- Kitchen areas - see Catering, page 108.
- Restaurant - also see Catering.
- Bedrooms: injury when lifting or moving furniture; sharp corners or edges of furniture.
- Use of portable electrical equipment such as vacuum cleaners; faulty or damaged equipment; guests' own appliances.
- Bar areas - see Pubs and bars, page 110.
- Office and reception areas - see Office-based businesses, page 92.
- Grounds: injuries from vehicles on site, including guests' and delivery of goods.
- Ground maintenance such as grass cutting - electrical equipment and need for circuit breakers; flying debris; trailing wires; broken glass or other sharp objects.
- Maintenance of buildings - see also use of ladders and equipment in Window Cleaners (page 106) and Carpenters and joiners (page 104).

Health

- Manual handling injuries from moving heavy or awkward loads.
- Use of cleaning and other hazardous substances; effects on skin/eyes/breathing/digestive system; danger of mixing chemicals; use of pesticides or other preparations.
- Potential for legionnaire's disease in water storage tanks/cooling systems.

- Smoking, especially for staff in areas where the public is allowed to smoke; appropriate and adequate ventilation systems required.

Fire

- Smoking by staff or customers, with discarded cigarettes or matches.
- Combustible materials as fuel, with soft furnishings, bedding, table linen; warning systems in storerooms.
- Heating systems and potential for explosion.
- Faulty or damaged electrical equipment; overloaded sockets; overloading with infrequent events causing extra drain on power, such as entertainment/shows/discos.
- Smouldering debris and bonfires in grounds.
- Potential for arson.

Take note

It is particularly important to consider these issues in relation to staff, contractors, entertainers, casual workers and guests.

Pubs and bars

Safety

- Crush injuries from handling barrels, kegs, crates, other containers.
- Working in confined spaces – cellars, especially danger of leaked carbon dioxide from cylinders.
- Burns from frosted cylinders; scalds from glass-washing machines when opened.
- Cuts from broken glass, bottles, other containers.
- Electric shock – use of portable electrical equipment; faulty or damaged equipment and cables; overloaded sockets; wet floors and surfaces near equipment.
- Slips and trips – trailing cables; obstructions in passageways and storage areas; inadequate storage facilities and space; wet or greasy floors; poor floor surfaces, steps and stairs; inadequate lighting or guarding of open areas; falls into cellars and other hatch openings.
- Use of steps and ladders.
- Violence – major concern especially late at night; when staff leave or enter premises; paying in to bank; avoid workers being left alone in bar areas with customers; violence can be from other staff as well as customers. System required for dealing with violence and notifying the Police or emergency services.

Health

- Smoking – whether as individuals or as the effects from other people smoking; ventilation systems vital, and properly considered smoking policy.
- Manual handling injuries from use of hazardous substances, including cleaning materials, pipe-cleaning fluids, ammonia-based products.
- Noise levels in bars, whether taped or live music.
- Hypodermic syringes of customers, and potential contamination.

Fire

- LPG cylinders, kegs and pressurised vessels or systems; danger of explosion.
- Alcohol products as fuel, leading to rapid spread of fire.
- Faulty electrical equipment; overloading sockets.
- Open fires, burning wood or coal, as source of sparks and ignition.
- Smoking and discarded cigarettes or matches.
- Room heaters; potential for portable heaters to be overturned.
- Oil-fired boilers and systems.
- Rubbish, waste paper and other scrap materials piled up; potential for arson.

Vehicle repairs

Safety

- Working in pit areas, confined spaces; (pits to be phased out in favour of lifts).

- Insecure hoists, jacks and other lifting gear – need for regular checks and maintenance; falling objects.

- Use of pressure equipment, radiator pressure caps, etc.

- Faulty portable electrical equipment; overloaded sockets; wrong fuses; danger of shock, especially in wet conditions.

- Slips and trips – trailing cables and hoses; damaged floor surfaces; debris on floor and work areas; spilt oil and grease, especially combined with water.

- Potential injury from use of machines and tools, including grinding, sanding, cutting; moving parts in engines when exposed.

- Customer safety on site; hazards from vehicles in motion, especially if drivers unfamiliar with site or vehicle.

- Acids and alkalis – brakes, battery acid, etc. Need for correct gloves and PPE.

- Adhesives and sealants, danger of severe skin damage.

- Air-bag units contain gas generators.

Health

- Some fumes heavier than air, likely to settle in lower sheltered levels, e.g. pits.

- Exhaust fumes from vehicles.

- Potential for skin cancers from use of grease and mineral oils; dermatitis and similar from adhesives and solvents; also act as sensitisers to later reactions.

- Breathing fumes from welding and other processes.

- Manual handling injuries from working in awkward, crouched conditions; lifting and pushing heavy loads.

- Noise from some tools and processes.

- Dangers to eyes from flying debris, falling rust, etc. when underneath vehicles, splashes of chemicals; need for adequate light at point of work.

- Radiation damage from welding or use of lasers.

- Asbestos in brake and clutch linings – OK in normal usage, but exposure when drilling, grinding or filing them.

> There must be adequate washing facilities, correct cleaning preparations, and barrier creams.

Fire

- Flammable substances, solvents, paints, adhesives, etc.

- Smoking and discarded cigarettes or matches; explosion hazard if residual fumes on clothing or hands after certain processes.

- Oil rags potential source of ignition – must be in fire-resistant containers, and only kept in small quantities.

- Sparks from electrical equipment, welding.

- Explosion risk from gas bottles and cylinders, LPG, pressure equipment.

- Petrol and oil as fire risk. Petrol must not be syphoned by mouth or used as cleaning agent!

Engineering

See also <u>Vehicle repairs</u>.

Safety

- **Injury from moving parts** of machinery – unguarded or disabled safety features; worn machinery, short-term fixing instead of proper maintenance.

- **Pressure vessels** and steam plant.

- **During use of hoists and other lifting gear**; hazards of falling objects, or swinging beams or loads.

- **Fork-lift trucks** and trolleys to move heavy items around workplace – need for proper training, controlled access, clearly marked pedestrian routes.

- **Slips and trips** – trailing cables, leads, air hoses, obstructions, poor floor surfaces and inadequate lighting.

- **Falls from heights**, ladders, stairs, open shaft or pit areas unfenced; proper use of ladders (see <u>Window cleaners</u>, p.108).

- **Working in confined spaces**, e.g. tanks or tanker bodies, pits, etc. - ventilation and escape routes vital; correct PPE to be worn, and rescue harnesses.

- **Electric shock** from faulty electrical equipment; overloading sockets; no circuit breakers in use.

- **Hand/arm vibration damage** from use of some tools or equipment.

- **Burns, eye damage** or piercing from flying particles during welding process.

Health

- **Exhaust fumes** from vehicles moving on site, including fork-lift trucks.

- **Noise** especially from machines in use; correct use of PPE hearing protection.

- **Extremes of heat or cold**; need for adequate ventilation and exhaust systems, properly maintained.

- **RSI** and repetitive twisting movements with some tasks; manual handling injuries from lifting, pushing or pulling big, heavy or awkward loads.

- **Fumes** or dusts from processes; radiation hazards, and need to identify particularly vulnerable groups of people that need protection.

- **Exposure to substances** that can cause damage or act as sensitisers, e.g. acids and alkalis; adhesives; oils, solvents and degreasing agents; CO_2 poisoning.

- **Need for adequate washing** and rest facilities, with correct cleaning substances and barrier creams.

- **Stress** – heavy workload, shift patterns, insufficient breaks, high noise levels.

Fire

- **Potential ignition sources** from sparks; static electricity; friction; oxyacetylene and welding sparks.

- **Electrical faults**; overloaded sockets; damaged cables.

- **Explosion risk** from pressure vessels or pressurised containers, including aerosol sprays.

- **Explosion** and rapid spread of fire from storage or use of chemical substances.

- **Dust** as explosion risk; poor ventilation.

- **Broken or disused pallets** stored next to building; risk of arson.

Glossary

Accident: an unexpected, unplanned event that leads to damage, harm or injury.

As far as reasonably practicable – action taken to control risks must be seen to be reasonable and proportionate to the level of risk, and cost of measures.

As far as practicable – action must be taken to control risk by whatever means are technically possible, without consideration of the cost of such action.

Controls: the range of controls in place to eliminate risk or reduce it.

EHO: Environmental Health Office, responsible for health and safety in lower-risk sectors, e.g. shops, offices, some leisure and care facilities, food businesses. They can cover a wider range of regulations than just H&S.

Hazard: something with the potential to cause harm or injury.

Hazard data sheets: statement provided by the supplier of any substance that may be hazardous (as defined by the Control of Substances Hazardous to Health [COSHH] regulations), providing information on the properties and harm likely if it is not used, stored, disposed of correctly. It also gives guidance on precautions to take when handling it plus remedial actions to take in the event of an emergency

Health and safety policy: a statement that outlines the company's views about health and safety, and commitment to taking necessary actions to safeguard workers from harm.

HSC: Health and Safety Commission, the tri-partite body representing workers, employers and legislators to define the way health and safety regulation must be put into practice.

HSE: Health and Safety Executive, the inspectors responsible for ensuring the regulations are followed and that legal action is taken if they are not. They carry out visits to workplaces (mainly high-risk sectors, e.g. manufacturing, construction, agriculture, vehicle trades) and provide a wide range of information and guidance literature.

Manual handling: relates to lifting, moving, holding, objects, materials, animals or people, particularly if the movements also include twisting the body or the person also has to reach outwards or upwards to complete the action.

OH&S: Occupational Health and Safety – refers to the legal framework within the UK where employers have a duty to protect the health, safety and well-being of people in the workplace.

OH&S MS: the whole system of processes, procedures, records and actions that are in place to make sure health, safety and fire risks are reduced as much as possible and managed effectively.

OH&S MSS: a formal management system for organising health and safety risks, the system usually monitored and certificated by a third party (an outside body that confirms the criteria of the standard have been met).

RIDDOR: Reporting of Injuries, Diseases, Dangerous Occurrences Regulations, i.e. notifying these things to HSE by phone, form or on-line.

Risk: the likelihood that something will actually cause harm or injury.

Risk assessment: the process of identifying hazards, assessing who could be affected and the type, severity of harm, and likelihood that it will occur.

Stakeholders: different groups of people who have an interest in the way business risks are managed, whether this is a personal or financial interest.

Safe System of Work: a formally documented system designed to ensure people are safe when carrying out specified tasks, it states how they must be carried out, what skills are needed by the operative, and all actions that **must** be carried out.

Index

www.ingramcontent.com/pod-product-compliance
Ingram Content Group UK Ltd.
Pitfield, Milton Keynes, MK11 3LW, UK
UKHW050129280225
455677UK00013B/292